WRITERS AND THEIR WORK

ISOBEL ARMSTRONG
General Editor

BRYAN LOUGHREY
Advisory Editor

J. R. R. Tolkien

J. R. R. TOLKIEN

WWV

J. R. R. Tolkien

Charles Moseley

Northcote House
in association with
The British Council

© Copyright 1997 by Charles Moseley

First published in 1997 by Northcote House Publishers Ltd, Plymbridge House, Estover Road, Plymouth PL6 7PY, United Kingdom.
Tel: +44 (01752) 202368 Fax: +44 (01752) 202330.

British Library Cataloguing-in-Publication Data
A catalogue record for this book is available from the British Library

ISBN 0 7463 0749 7

Typeset by PDQ Typesetting, Newcastle-under-Lyme
Printed and bound in the United Kingdom

Contents

Acknowledgements

The long road to the writing of this short book started many years ago. A group of us, undergraduates just into our irresponsible tweens, were on a reading and walking holiday in the English Lake District with the Dean of Queens' College, Cambridge, Henry St. J. Hart. We sat around a fire in a Homely House as the snow piled up in the January dark outside, and read *The Hobbit*; and followed it, over the next terms, with the reading of *The Lord of the Rings*. Tolkien's myth became for us a way of saying, and it seemed only proper that he himself should visit the group and read to us from the story of Beren and Lúthien. The first of my debts, then, is a personal one to that group of friends, now 'somdeel stape in age', to Henry Hart, and to J. R. R. Tolkien.

But there are many others. West's indispensable bibliography shows how many have reaped the field before me; as Chaucer once put it, 'I come after, glenyng here and there'. My major debt, which I am only too willing to acknowledge, is to the work of Humphrey Carpenter, both in his biography of Tolkien and in his collection of the correspondence. The penetrating study of the man and his work by Tom Shippey was a big influence on my thinking. The work of critics of often radical persuasions has stimulated me to rethink a lot of the certainties that accumulate after a long time of familiarity with an author, and my Bibliography makes clear my debt to some often seminal work.

But there are other, personal, debts too, to people who have put up with me in the period of gestation when they were plagued by my unaccountable whims. So thanks are certainly due to Mary O'Keeffe, who in the middle of her impossibly busy job as Librarian and Housemistress at The Leys School, Cambridge, somehow found time to help me with the job of trawling from the

Internet a finding list of material to be examined; Dr Bryan Loughrey, Director of Research at the Roehampton Institute, and Advisory Editor of this series, who first asked me to consider writing this book, and always showed a concerned interest in it; Brian Hulme of Northcote House, whose patience and understanding made my life a great deal easier; my wife, who has once again put up with the disruption that the itch of writing brings to an ordered life; and, very warmly, I recognize my obligation to Christina Zaba, whose impeccable editing made this a much better book than it would otherwise have been. The faults and errors that remain are certainly mine.

Biographical Outline

1892	Born at Bloemfontein, South Africa.
1895	Returns with mother and younger brother to England: business keeps father behind (dies 1896).
1896–1900	Residence at Sarehole Mill, Birmingham.
1900	Move to Moseley. Mrs Tolkien becomes a Roman Catholic. JRRT attends King Edward VI School, Birmingham for just under two years; after an interlude at St Philip's grammar school, Edgbaston, returns there, with a scholarship, in September 1903.
1904	Mrs Tolkien dies of diabetes.
1908	First meeting with Edith Bratt, while lodging with Mrs Faulkner.
1909	JRRT fails to win a scholarship to Oxford. Association with Edith Bratt discovered by Fr. Francis Morgan, friend, patron, and financial support for the two boys. Tolkien forbidden to communicate with her until he is 21.
1910	JRRT wins Exhibition to Exeter College, Oxford.
1911	Visit to Switzerland. Goes up to Oxford (October).
1913	Renews association with Edith Bratt. Switches from Classical course to English Language and Literature.
1914	Engagement to Edith after her conversion to Roman Catholicism.
1915	First Class Honours in final examinations. Commissioned in Lancashire Fusiliers.
1916	Marriage to Edith. Service in France. Takes part in Battle of the Somme. Invalided home in November with trench fever.

1917	Convalescing, he begins to write the 'Book of Lost Tales', which later develops into the *Silmarillion*. Birth of eldest son (John).
1918	Returns to Oxford with his family to take up post on the New English Dictionary.
1920	Reader in English Language at University of Leeds. Birth of son Michael.
1922	Works with E. V. Gordon on edition of *Sir Gawain and the Green Knight* (published 1925).
1924	Professor of English Language at Leeds. Birth of Christopher.
1924	Elected to Rawlinson and Bosworth Chair of Anglo-Saxon at University of Oxford.
1926	Becomes friendly with C. S. Lewis. Formation of group – the Coalbiters – to read through the Old Norse sagas in the original language. (This task complete in the early 1930s, a similar group, the Inklings, forms to meet, hear, and discuss each other's writing.)
1929	Birth of daughter Priscilla.
1930?	Begins to write *The Hobbit*.
1936	Lecture on '*Beowulf*: The Monsters and the Critics'. Incomplete *Hobbit* read by Allen and Unwin.
1937	Completion and publication of *The Hobbit, or There and Back Again*. Stanley Unwin suggests he should write a sequel. Beginning of *The Lord of the Rings*.
1939	Lecture in University of St Andrews, 'On Fairy Stories'. Charles Williams moves to Oxford and joins the Inklings.
1945	Elected Merton Professor of English Language and Literature at University of Oxford.
1949	Completion of *LR*. Publication of *Farmer Giles of Ham*.
1952	*LR* accepted by Allen and Unwin.
1953	Verse drama, *The Homecoming of Beorhtnoth, Beorhthelm's Son*, published (in existence by 1945).
1954	Publication of *The Fellowship of the Ring* and *The Two Towers*.
1955	Publication of *The Return of the King*.
1959	Retires from professorship.
1962	Publication of *The Adventures of Tom Bombadil*.

1964	Publication of *Tree and Leaf*, containing the revised version of 'On Fairy Stories' and a short story, 'Leaf by Niggle'.
1965	Pirated American version of *LR*. Immense popularity of *LR* in American universities and colleges.
1967	Publication of *Smith of Wootton Major*. Creation of *The Road goes ever on: A Song Cycle* with music by Donald Swann.
1968	Removal to Poole.
1971	Edith Tolkien dies.
1972	JRRT returns to Oxford. Honoured by CBE and Oxford's Hon. Litt. D.
1973	Dies in Bournemouth.

Works Appearing Posthumously

1975	Translation of *Sir Gawain and the Green Knight, Pearl and Sir Orfeo*, ed. with a preface by Christopher Tolkien.
1977	*The Silmarillion*, ed. Christopher Tolkien. Records issued of readings of parts of the book. Exhibition of JRRT's drawings at the Ashmolean Museum, Oxford.
1980	*Unfinished Tales of Númenor and Middle Earth*, ed. Christopher Tolkien.
1981	*Letters of JRRT*, ed. Humphrey Carpenter with the assistance of Christopher Tolkien.
1982	*Mr Bliss* (from JRRT's illustrated MS) and *Finn and Hengest: The Fragment and the Episode*, ed. Alan Bliss.
1983	*The Book of Lost Tales I*, ed. Christopher Tolkien.
1984	*The Book of Lost Tales 2*, ed. Christopher Tolkien.
1985	*The Lays of Beleriand*, ed. Christopher Tolkien.
1986	*The Shaping of Middle Earth*, ed. Christopher Tolkien.
1987	*The Lost Road and Other Writings: Language and Legend before 'The Lord of the Rings'*, ed. Christopher Tolkien.

Abbreviations and References

Carpenter   Humphrey Carpenter, *J. R. R. Tolkien: A
                     Biography* (London, 1977).
JRRT   J. R. R. Tolkien.
LR   *The Lord of the Rings* (London, 1954–5).
Letters   ed. Humphrey Carpenter, with the assist-
                     ance of Christopher Tolkien, *Letters of
                     J. R. R. Tolkien: A Selection* (London, 1981).
'Monsters and Critics'   J. R. R. Tolkien, '*Beowulf*: The Monsters
                     and the Critics', *Proceedings of the British
                     Academy*, 22 (1936), 245–95.

Introduction

Tolkien's fiction sharply divides opinion. Readers of extreme learning and sophistication, and of none, admire *The Lord of the Rings* and *The Hobbit*. An apparently insatiable demand for more led to the publication, during and after Tolkien's lifetime, of an enormous volume of material supplementary to these books. At the same time, many people, from exactly the same sorts of backgrounds, found them unreadable.

Tolkien was not originally writing for a mass audience. Yet his work achieved what might be called cult status for many, despite their differing sharply from him in education and in cultural and political stances. For many who were young in the 1960s, his books seemed to offer a myth with which to interpret reality. Widely translated, they won the accolade of parody; his characters were taken into pop art and their names adopted by rock bands; his work spawned many imitators, and is an important progenitor of modern fantasy fiction. 'Tolkien' became a successful marketing operation – one which Tolkien himself regarded with some ambivalence. Furthermore, his work still generates much critical and scholarly debate, from the standpoints of numerous critical persuasions; and while 'Frodo and the Hobbits' rocked away into oblivion, Frodo and his world were discussed at several international scholarly conferences, their *Proceedings* filling large volumes.

The books sustaining this unusual cultural phenomenon present problems. Classifying them as 'fantasy', which is common practice, begs many questions, though it is difficult to know what other term to use. For, since Tolkien wrote, and partly because of him, 'fantasy' has acquired a range of meanings: to some, it means no more than lurid covers enclosing more lurid stories, or video games; while others, like

Todorov, Hunter, Irwin, Jackson, or Swinfen, have explored it theoretically as an important genre with its own rhetoric. Tom Shippey, one of the most perceptive of Tolkien's critics, points out that fantasy's roots lie in the beginning of European literature. In its broadest definition it would include everything from the *Odyssey* to *Beowulf* to *Cinderella* to Terry Pratchett: it 'makes deliberate use of something known to be impossible', or, as C. S. Lewis put it in *An Experiment in Criticism* (1961), 'impossibles and preternaturals'. (What is 'known to be impossible' may, of course, vary according to time and place.) Modern fantasy (including science fiction) may be seen as a way of making imaginative space in the face of scientific advance and the spread of the scientific imagination. But unlike science fiction, which is premissed on the possible eventual continuity of the everyday world with that described, fantasy asserts the impregnable otherness. Moreover, fantasy need not follow the conventions of the novel as it has developed in this century, and may, indeed, invite revision of those conventions.

Yet, even ignoring the conventions of the novel, Tolkien's books have serious flaws. One may put on one side the fact that the ideological positions encoded in them even admirers might find untenable or repellent, for the merits of any book do not depend on its agreeing with readers' assumptions – I do not need to worship Zeus to read Homer with profit. But the writing can be slack and clichéd, the narratorial voice uncertain. Characterization is colourless by comparison with what Tolkien's contemporaries and predecessors could do. The few females remain ciphers seen from an almost wholly male perspective, one which is, apparently endorsed by the books. The imagined world is vast in scale but limited in depth, and partially incoherent. There are also demonstrable merits, if not fashionable ones. Judged by the criteria of the epic, or the romance, or the folk tale, where narrative is central, the stories stand up well: and these types of writing, of course, were central to Tolkien's interests as a scholar. (Indeed, the *Iliad* or *Beowulf* exhibit many of the faults mentioned above.) Some readers can experience, as in reading Malory (to whom Tolkien was compared by Naomi Mitchison in the initial publicity for *LR*), a peculiar sense of living temporarily in another world, another historical continuum. Here, perhaps, lies one explanation for his appeal. Hence, also, might arise the criticism of his work as escapist, distracting people from problems of a real world much more complicated than his fiction describes, and for the description and analysis of which tools exist that were not available to Homer or the *Beowulf* poet.

Authors may be as unreliable as anyone else about their work. But how Tolkien said he understood the business of writing is at least interesting. This study will suggest, firstly, that Tolkien's critical and philological work, and his theory of story, illuminates his fiction. For example, he thought hard about language and its development, and how it implies and constructs a culture. This concern surfaces in the linguistic games and self-referential literary/scholarly pastiche in his work. He interested himself, too, in the nature of fiction, its place in society, and its appeal to individuals. He was also a devout Christian. From this background grew a philosophy of literature, shared with friends like Lewis, which challenges some now orthodox critical theory; a philosophy which, in other times, has had impressive support. Secondly, I shall examine connections between the major stories, and their status not as free-standing wholes but as parts of an unfinished and unfinishable myth, to which Tolkien was deeply committed emotionally: a myth which expressed some of his fears about the world he experienced and the England he loved, and one which many accepted as a map of their own fears.

1

The Man

In June 1972 the University of Oxford conferred on Tolkien the honorary degree of Doctor of Letters. Outside Oxford he was known best as the author of *The Hobbit* and the book that followed it in the 1950s, *The Lord of the Rings*. The books had made him a rich man, and were already spawning those telling indications of wide readership, imitations and parodies. But despite courteous references to *The Hobbit* and to the still-unpublished *Silmarillion* in the Latin address by the Public Orator, it was clear that his peers were honouring Tolkien not for his fiction but for his philological work. This was no slight of him as a creative writer: rather, it recognized the value of his scholarly work, that some of his publications were landmarks in the study of the ancient languages and literatures of Northern Europe. The University judged wisely, for Tolkien's linguistic researches lie at the heart of what drove the writing of the books that make up what many now refer to as 'Tolkien' – the author's name standing for his writings as does 'Milton', or 'Wordsworth' or 'Conrad', in a way that indicates acceptance into some sort of canon.

Language, the web of words, is what holds societies together: to explain a word you need to understand the language, and to explain the language, you need to understand the society that used it. Language and words, the naming of things, is the most central human activity; it was, according to legend, Adam's first. Language allows us to live together, to make some sort of sense of our world: to *make* our world, indeed. There is no division between Tolkien's philology and his fiction. The history recorded in *LR* and its related texts is, in the end, secondary to the invented languages that Tolkien developed it to explain: 'A language requires a suitable habitation, and a history in which it can develop' (Letter, 9 February 1967, *Letters* p. 375). So Tolkien's ideas about language, and about the nature of story, are helpful in understanding what he was doing in one of the most extraordinary bodies of modern fiction.

His mother's family, the Suffields, originally from the fat Worcestershire countryside Tolkien idealized both in fact and in the golden picture he drew of the Shire and the Little Kingdom, were impoverished Birmingham merchants. In 1891, Mabel Suffield married Arthur Tolkien. The Tolkiens, originally from Saxony, had been English for several generations. That family told (as families do) stories of past glory, such as that of a noble ancestor who with high courage captured the standard of the Turkish Sultan at the siege of Vienna in 1683. But Arthur Tolkien, less romantically, went to manage a bank in Bloemfontein, South Africa, where his elder child, John Ronald Reuel Tolkien, was born in 1892.

In 1895 worsening health forced mother and children to return to England. Tolkien never knew his father, who died in 1896, leaving little provision for his widow and family. Mrs Tolkien rented a cottage near Sarehole Mill, then outside Birmingham, where Tolkien spent what he remembered as four of his happiest years. But in 1900 the Grahamesque Golden Age ended. Mabel Tolkien, to the horror of her Anglican and Unitarian relations, turned Roman Catholic; and thereafter they stopped the little financial help they had been giving her. Seeking cheaper lodgings and a congenial Catholic pastorate, the family moved to Moseley, an inner suburb of Birmingham. Ronald Tolkien began to attend King Edward VI School, where, except for a short spell at St Philip's Grammar School in Edgbaston, he remained until he left for Oxford in 1911.

Mabel Tolkien, a gifted linguist, educated her sons herself in Latin and French, in drawing, in calligraphy, and in botany. That early training told in the interest in languages Tolkien showed at King Edward's. Latin and Greek were common accomplishments, since they formed the core of the curriculum in English Public Schools then and for long afterwards. Not so common, perhaps, was the sensuous enjoyment of the sound and structure of Greek which Tolkien recalled himself feeling. Even less common was Tolkien's determination to master Anglo-

Saxon – Middle English, its descendant, he took in his stride – and the extinct Gothic. (A letter to W. H. Auden, 7 June 1955, *Letters*, p. 213), describes his facility for languages and how he 'took to early west-midland Middle English *as a known tongue* as soon as I set eyes on it' – italics mine.) Few school debating societies – even those occasionally holding debates in Latin – can have included a member who, posing as a Greek Ambassador to the Roman Senate, harangued it in Greek, or as a Barbarian envoy in Gothic, and on another occasion spoke fluent Anglo-Saxon. But in all this brilliance, in this delight in the different worlds different languages signify, one can discern some foundations of the later fiction. Already, too, Tolkien was inventing his own private languages, with a passion, resourcefulness, and commitment which took time from the studies on which depended his winning of a scholarship to Oxford. Without such success, boys of Tolkien's economic background simply had no chance of an education at one of the older universities.

Mrs Tolkien's death from diabetes in 1904 affected her sons deeply. Already her elder son had developed a passionate attachment to the Roman Catholic Church like her, and her will appointed as guardian of the boys her parish priest and friend, Father Francis Xavier Morgan, a stern but generous and affectionate man. The boys had to move into lodgings, and while in rooms Father Morgan found for them near the Birmingham Oratory, Ronald Tolkien fell in love with a fellow lodger, Edith Bratt. Undoubtedly Father Morgan attributed Tolkien's failure to win a scholarship in 1908 to the association with Edith, and made him promise not to see or communicate with her until he was 21. That promise was kept. On the morning of his twenty-first birthday, in 1913, he contacted Edith again, and persuaded her to marry him. In 1914, after her reception into the Church – an important condition – they were engaged, and married in 1916 just before he embarked for the Western Front.

In 1910 Tolkien won the lesser award of an Exhibition. Though worth less than the expected Scholarship, it was still enough for an undergraduate to live on if careful and frugal. (Not many manage to be both for all three years.) In 1911, after visiting Switzerland, from which a souvenir postcard survives, noted in Tolkien's handwriting 'Origin of Gandalf', he went up to Exeter

College. His performance in Classics was unremarkable, and in 1913 he switched to reading English. But more important than any formal course were what the College Library and the Bodleian Library offered the inquisitive mind. At Oxford he explored Welsh seriously for the first time; its musical beauty greatly influenced nomenclature in his fictions. Even more significant was the discovery of Finnish, a language unrelated to any other in Europe save Magyar and Samoyed. Years before he had read the Everyman translation of the *Kalevala*, the mass of unsystematic legends – a 'primitive undergrowth of literature', as he said in a paper read to a College society – collected by Elias Lönnrot from the oral peasant tradition in Finland and published in his final version of fifty cantos in 1850. Its ill-fated heroes, its story of the forging of the mysterious Sampo, had captivated him, but he had not gone far in the extraordinarily difficult language which, for example, has fourteen cases. Now he did: it influenced his Quenya language, which he would one day give his Elves. Since his invented languages had hitherto been basically Germanic, this marks a major change in direction. Moreover, the pattern of Finnish verse dictated by the stress in Finnish commonly falling on the first syllable of the word is echoed in the verses in Elvish in *LR*. (Longfellow's *Hiawatha* is in the nearest English equivalent to the metre of the *Kalevala*.)

When war came in 1914 he decided to finish his degree before enlisting. Having won the expected First Class in finals, he was commissioned in the Lancashire Fusiliers. So much has been written about the horrors of the Somme offensive of 1916 in which Tolkien fought, with its 20,000 dead on the first day, that summary is unnecessary. He was one of the fortunate ones: he survived, and was lucky enough to have recurrent trench fever badly enough to be invalided to various parts of England until the Armistice. In the second edition of *LR*, Tolkien remarks, 'By 1918 all but one of my close friends were dead': men with whom he had grown up from boyhood at school, and whom he had known in the spring of their days at Oxford. Such loss leaves permanent scars, which sometimes never heal. To those of us who have not been through such travail, the experiences of those who saw Hell in France are, in the end, incommunicable, and it is presumptuous to write about them. All one can say is that for Tolkien, as for many of his generation, the War was one of the defining things: its ghosts haunted the long years that lay ahead, and framed the vision of the new.

Yet life did go on. Men did return, and take up their lives again. They could do nothing else. The ploughman returned to his plough, the scholar to his library. The changes took place, as Conrad put it in *Heart of Darkness*, 'inside'. Tolkien returned to a new son, to a wife with whom so far he had shared no domesticity, to the need to earn a living. A job on the *New English Dictionary* in Oxford allowed him to do what he loved and what he was best at – researching the family trees of words, their original forms, and their earliest contexts and contents. It was a job for which, in fact, he had trained himself: while other children often invent private languages – 'private lang.' was his abbreviation for the 'adolescent' pursuit out of which we may be grateful he never grew – Tolkien's was unusual in that he invented a word, and then reasoned from his knowledge of the rules of linguistic change what its *earlier* forms *must have* been. Such thinking was now as natural as breathing, and anybody who has begun to explore language in this perspectived way must be aware that such looking back glimpses lost worlds that once were real with noise and blood and laughter and sunlight. Once, the Gothic root of a common word was spoken by people of like passions with us.

The *Dictionary* was an admirable stepping stone to a regular academic career; first (1920) as Reader, then (1924) Professor, in English Language at the University of Leeds, then rapidly back to Oxford that same year to the Rawlinson and Bosworth Chair of Anglo-Saxon. And there Tolkien stayed, teaching with distinction, managing with aplomb (and apparent enjoyment) the politicking in a School that for many years had been split between those, medievalists and philologists, who saw the academic study of literature as primarily a matter of philology, archaeology, and history, and were not interested in much after Chaucer, and those enthusiasts for later writings who made disturbing claims about the moral value of literature. (Tolkien played a significant part in this grumbling storm in a rather important teacup.) The Merton Professorship was given him in 1945, and generations of undergraduates, not all reading his subjects, took from his crowded lectures things that he cannot have known he had given them. A don's life – and he was (apparently) living in all respects a don's life – in the eyes of the big world, is sequestered, comfortable, even self-indulgent. The reality is that, lived properly, it is full of passion, in confrontation with the knottiest problems of all, of who we are and what (if anything) we are for, and how we can talk about it – and with the crucial business of the teaching of the young of the tribe. There can hardly be a more important job.

Appearances, however, did not reveal all. Some distinguished scholarship appeared, some as papers and articles, some as major editions. In 1925, for example, Tolkien edited with E. V. Gordon the late-Fourteenth-century poem *Sir Gawain and the Green Knight* which put the study of that poem and its relatives on a wholly new footing. That edition remains, in its revised edition by Norman Davis (1968), the basis for serious study of the poem. But colleagues did wonder why Professor Tolkien was so dilatory in producing the work they expected. The reason was that he had a secret life. Just as at school he found the secret world of his 'private lang.' more fascinating than the work that had to get him that Oxford Award, so at Oxford he retired into the invented world to which those trails of words led him, which finally came to be almost as real as the one in which the hated motor cars coughed their way up Headington Hill. Only now, years after his death, does the mass of unfinished, sometimes inchoate, material published from his papers reveal just how huge was his fictional output.

By 1917, convalescing, he had begun the earliest version of *The Book of Lost Tales*. Much revised, it eventually became *The Silmarillion*. As everywhere else, Tolkien was an indefatigable reviser (like his own character Niggle), ever unwilling to let go of a piece of writing, always prone to rewrite the lot when a publisher had simply asked him to check the punctuation. *The Silmarillion*, from this earliest version to the latest (eventually published in 1977), has fair claim to be regarded as his basic work, dominating his creative thinking from at least 1917 to his death in 1973. Its great length describes, in a series of more or less chronologically successive chapters, Ilúvatar's creation of a Universe, the entry of evil into it, and the suffering and strife and heroism and glory of consequent events. It is the Old Testament to the New of *LR* – prehistory, the Genesis, the Fall, the Exodus of the Noldor, the wars against Melkor/Morgoth, the rise and fall of the Kingdom of Men called Númenor, and finally the narrative of the Rings of Power from which *LR* stems. Everything he wrote relates to it, either directly, in the case of *The Hobbit*, *The Adventures of Tom Bombadil* and *LR*, or thematically, in the cases of *Farmer Giles of Ham* and *Smith of Wootton Major*. One might also argue that the understanding of language and fiction which informs his critical writings is affected greatly by the experience of building and living in the edifice of *The Silmarillion*.

But in the 1930s few knew of this activity, though Tolkien had read some stories to an audience – for example, in 1920 he read 'The Fall of Gondolin' to an Exeter College society including Hugo Dyson and Nevill Coghill. Nothing had been printed. Sometime after 1930 Tolkien, marking School Certificate exam papers, suddenly found a sentence in his mind, which he jotted down on the back of a script: 'In a hole in the ground there lived a hobbit'. That curious beginning, with its echo of Kenneth Grahame's *The Wind in the Willows*, was the genesis of *The Hobbit, or There and Back Again*, read to the children, but left unfinished. In 1932 C. S. Lewis, with whom Tolkien had become friendly in 1926, read this incomplete manuscript; Tolkien also read it to 'The Inklings'– Lewis, the novelist and poet Charles Williams, Hugo Dyson, Owen Barfield, and others – who met weekly to read each other's work. Word of it got about; still incomplete, it was read by Allen and Unwin. The enthusiasm of Rayner Unwin, the young son of the Chairman of the firm, whose opinion was sought on all children's book manuscripts led to Allen and Unwin offering to publish; and its success, (in 1937), led Stanley Unwin to encourage Tolkien to write a sequel. So Tolkien offered him the incomplete, unregularized mass of manuscripts that became *The Silmarillion*: the only thing in more or less coherent form appears to have been the verse version of *Beren and Lúthien the Elfmaiden*. But Stanley Unwin, while praising bits of it as 'wonderful', rejected it, and repeated his request for a sequel to *The Hobbit*.

The Hobbit, the story of Bilbo Baggins's unexpected journey with a group of dwarves to recover their lost kingdom beneath the Lonely Mountain, is readily classifiable as a quest adventure, like many 'fairy stories', with a happy ending. Rayner Unwin's report, quoted by Carpenter (*Letters*, p. 184) can hardly be bettered as a summary and as a glimpse of how easily a child might accept the plausibility of invented creatures like wargs and hobbits:

> Bilbo Baggins was a hobbit who lived in his hobbit hole and *never* went for adventures, at last Gandalf the wizard and his dwarves persuaded him to go. He had a very exiting time fighting goblins and wargs. at last they got to the lonley mountain; Smaug, the dragon who gawreds it is killed and after a terrific battle with the goblins he returned home – rich! This book, with the help of maps, does not need any illustrations it is good and should appeal to all children between the ages of 5 and 9.

(No irony, perhaps, in the fact that young Mr Unwin was ten.)

LR, anticipated as the 'new *Hobbit*', was no such thing. The quest of Frodo the Hobbit to destroy the Ring of Power that Bilbo had found in *The Hobbit* is the heart of a complex narrative with many characters, and it raises important issues of personal and political morality. The quest, eventually successful, does not restore any *status quo ante*: rather, the book is suffused with a pessimism which sees all outcomes as painful. The book can be seen as a study of a final loss of innocence, and Tolkien became very emotionally involved with it. Moreover, the book explicitly connects with and develops *The Silmarillion*'s cycle of stories (on which work had not stopped) that as yet had had no audience. In 1952, Allen and Unwin, daunted by the size of *LR*, decided to split the six books into three volumes, and, doubting more than modest commercial success, agreed with Tolkien terms giving him no return until the book was in profit, when he would get 50 per cent of the profits. Few agreements made with such trepidation can have made an author so rich, for the books – *The Fellowship of the Ring* and *The Two Towers* (1954), and *The Return of the King* (1955) – were extremely successful.

This success came late. The other life still had to be led. There were lectures on Old and Middle English, Old Norse, and related topics to be delivered. The burden of teaching continued: never enough time to do anything, never enough time for the academic papers and books everyone expected. In 1936, *The Hobbit* abandoned, Tolkien gave the lecture 'Beowulf: The Monsters and the Critics', which redefined the terms of debate for that poem, and is still, sixty years later, one of the seminal discussions of it. In 1939 the Andrew Lang lecture in the University of St Andrews, 'On Fairy Stories', deployed Tolkien's immense scholarship in a reasoned plea in defence of mythopoeic narrative. In 1962 the Early English Text Society published, after many delays on his part, his edition of *Ancrene Wisse: The English Text of the Ancrene Riwle*. He had long before recognized that the author of this important manual of instruction for a group of anchoresses was aware of the full resources of a literary language of great antiquity of which few examples remained. But though important, these works were a small output for one in his position. For his inner world drew on the world of the scholar – could not, indeed, have grown without it – but in the end it made different claims on him. He was a man divided. On the one hand was the scholar, the analyst, the critic; on the other, he was constantly distracted from such study by the attraction of fiction, of making worlds of words. Tolkien was the schoolboy neglecting his Greek and Latin for the delight of 'private lang.'; the young don turning in the small hours from that which keeps his family to the growing universe his mind is bringing into being; the old professor aware of this tension in himself and, ironically, when he did publish his fiction, masking himself as editor, commentator, historian. He was constantly being seduced, like Thomas the Rymer in the old ballad, into the Land of Faerye whence he returned to tell of strange sights.

Tolkien might have been uneasy about a book about him in a series called 'Writers and their Work'. In his view, biography and literary criticism were entirely separate. Humphrey Carpenter ruefully records his remark, 'Investigation of an author's biography is an entirely vain and false approach to his works': those works must stand alone, within the context they create, not by virtue of explanations derived from their author's biography. Indeed, with the ancient books that occupied Tolkien's professional life, biography was impossible, since no details of their authors survived. He writes to W. H. Auden (February 1966: *Letters*, p. 367) 'I regret very much' that Auden had 'contracted to write a book about me'. Yet Tolkien's life and work is full of contradiction: for few authors have been so ready to talk and write fluently, at great length, and clearly with some pleasure, to many types of correspondent about their fiction, about materials ancillary to it, and what they felt about it. There is, for example, the remarkable letter to Milton Waldman, of late

1951 (*Letters*, no. 131); there is also a long account to Auden (7 June 1955; *Letters*, p. 211–16) of the writing of *The Hobbit*, *LR*, and their place in Tolkien's creative activity, and the letter to Houghton Mifflin Co. of Boston, designed to be used for setting the public record straight, which he wrote on 30 June 1955 (*Letters*, p.218 ff.). But even in such letters (auto)biography is allowed to go only so far. He does not, save to his family, reveal his private self. There is an assertion, often implicit but occasionally explicit, that he *discovered* rather than created his stories, that they are part of a much larger and as yet unrevealed – undiscovered – whole, an implication that the author is passive, more an editor than a creator. Yet this reconstructing – re-authorizing – an account of the books' writing is to an unknowable extent fictional. And he can offer contradictory interpretations of what his work is about. Were there nothing else, his writings are a fascinating sidelight on how a remarkably alert mind thought about itself writing.

But there are things in his life (not least his concern with books where the death of the unknowable author took place long ago) which can illuminate the published narratives. Some of his views, like those of many of his generation, do bear on what turned up in his fiction. Three things are especially important: Tolkien's religion, the experience of the 1914–18 War, and the nature of Oxford academic life and society.

The Catholic discipline of frequent attendance at Mass and frequent confession structures not only the day, the week, and the cycle of the Church's year, with its calendar of saints' days, fast days, and the great festivals; it also shapes the way of seeing the self. Confession encourages self-analysis. It is based on the premise that man, created for glory, is a fallen being, constantly in need of the supernatural grace of forgiveness and renewal. Man, both 'poor potsherd' and 'immortal diamond', as Hopkins saw him, is a paradox, a divided self: St Paul diagnosed, most succinctly in Romans, 7, what we all know of ourselves. And while Christianity is pessimistic about man's propensity to evil, it is by definition optimistic about the constantly intervening grace of a God who, taking human nature on him, suffered as a man and forgives and remakes the broken. This envisages a creator who, not simply a watchmaker, loves his world, suffers in its sufferings, lives in it, and sustains it in life. Christianity offers, too, a model for understanding time, the world, suffering, death: it offers a teleology, a vision of history which is not meaningless or merely cyclic, but purposive, leading to some great end, the climax of all that has ever been or ever shall be. Briefly, it is a vision of a world fallen from its pristine beauty, but capable of being redeemed and remade by enormous sacrifice – not to its former state, for what is gone can never be recovered, but to some new glory. Hence everything is under ultimate judgement. Even so, as the fourteenth-century mystic Julian of Norwich said, 'all shall be well, and all manner of thing shall be well'.

A mind really believing this must accept that 'Good' and 'Evil' are not relative or subjective terms (merely, as A. J. Ayer famously remarked, other ways of saying 'Hurrah!' and 'Boo!'), but represent a fundamental divide in the Universe: and that the good is ultimately triumphant. Even so, evil may remain active and powerful, though, as St Augustine argued, it is nothing of itself, but simply a privation of Good, parasitic upon it. These views underlie all the fiction of Tolkien, Charles Williams, and Lewis. Moreover, this life is a pilgrimage, a passing through a varied countryside of beauty and ugliness to some, as yet unseen, destination which will give the whole journey purpose. A paradox follows: this world – England, the Shire, Eriador, Beleriand – is both enormously important (for it is our home, and reminds us of the lineaments of perfection) *and* intrinsically worthless (for it will vanish away when the heavens are rolled up like a curtain and there shall be no more sea). Now this sense of a damaged world, pointing beyond itself to what once was before the Fall (in Eä, in Valinor, in Eden) and to what shall unimaginably be (in Heaven, where all stories end, coming together in a final harmony) underlies all Tolkien's fiction and all his writing about fiction. He elaborates a theory that the storyteller creates a sub-world, but that sub-world is rooted in the story that is our world, and that in turn is rooted in a story which as yet we only glimpse. This is a very Neo-Platonic view of story: and it greatly affects how a writer can practise his art.

The Great War marked millions of men who survived. They saw their comrades die, often horribly. The war memorials of England, France, and Germany record the waste of young lives, the empty places at the family tables, the slow drawing down of blinds on the lives of young widows and orphans. Those who lived through it could, sometimes, talk: the boredom of much of it, the discomfort, the occasional humour, the luck of finding a bit of luxury, like some good tobacco when there seems no chance of any – just the atmosphere Tolkien evokes of the hours before, and after, the assault on Minas Tirith (*LR*, V, chs. 1, 4, 6, and 8; cf. III. ch. 8): and those who have been in battle say it is done well. But few talked easily of the loss of their friends, or of the horrors of the Flanders countryside turned to mud in the autumn rains, with bloated bodies sticking out of the side of the new trench that would be no defence against the next bombardment. This is the picture behind Tolkien's picture of Nirnaeth Arnoediad in *The Silmarillion*, of the Dead Marshes that Frodo and Sam and Gollum cross, and especially of the tortured, smoky Waste Land of Mordor, a landscape criss-crossed by military roads where columns of brutalized conscript troops march, aware of being used by a remote, incomprehensible High Command. On this plain, 'pocked with great holes, as if, while it was still a waste of soft mud, it had been smitten with a shower of bolts and slingstones' (*LR*, VI, ch. 3), 'writhing tangled brambles'... as tough as wire' with 'hooked barbs, that rent like knives' recall the barbed-wire entanglements of the Western Front; and only 'low scrubby trees...lurk and cling' (*LR*, VI, ch. 2). Trees were emotionally important to Tolkien; he had seen shelling make the lovely elms of Flanders matchwood, and even here, in Mordor, he uses verbs that suggest the scrubby trees are somehow active, with personality.

The brief hopes of the immediate post-war years were prelude only to further crisis: an unmanageable world economic system, indifferent to the lives it wrecked, and in the thirties the rise of a yet more terrible power in Hitler's Germany. Many felt that the war that came in 1939 could have been avoided had the Western allies acted resolutely earlier. That conflict, with the policies of terror-bombing of civilian targets, used by both sides in the end, gave the final *coup de grâce* to a world and a set of social assumptions that the Great War had already weakened dramatically: after 1945, when the concentration camps were liberated, revealing to what depths a noble and civilized nation in the heartland of European culture could fall, it was difficult to believe in the goodness and dignity of man. Some, indeed, explicitly saw the history of the previous thirty years in apocalyptic terms. For example, in Charles Williams's *The Descent of the Dove* (new edn. 1953, paperback 1963) the chronological table (p. 219) explicitly renames the First and Second World Wars in the context of Apocalypse.

This pessimistic vision affects all Tolkien's fiction. The comfortable, complacent (English) Shire is in a world moving to catastrophe. There is no hope *here*, the best that can be won is an interim before the dark: all chances in the War, for us as for Elrond, are fraught with loss and pain. But this pessimism, like Eliot's, is paradoxical: it is the pessimism of the St Augustine who wrote *The City of God* – 'here is no eternal city, here is no abiding stay' – but there is Hope, and resurrection, under the shadow of the Rock. It is noticeable that in the two narratives which seem to have meant most to Tolkien, the story of Beren and Lúthien and *LR*, Beren and Gandalf return from the dead. But the resurrected is not the same as the one who died.

Tolkien's social and academic world can, finally, illuminate things some readers find puzzling or objectionable: what has been called unkindly the *Boys' Own Paper* morality, and the portrayal of women.

The middle-class milieu of Tolkien's youth is now a fading memory, and it is difficult not to impose on our view of the past moral and ethical assumptions which are the product of our own very different society. A middle-class woman and a middle-class man were aware of and in large measure consented to social patterns and constraints which we should find intolerable. There were assumptions about what was proper to a woman and to a man in behaviour, duties, and obligations. There was an expectation on both sides of a marriage that a woman did not go out to work: if she did, it acknowledged that her husband could not discharge his duty to keep her and the family. There were assumptions about chastity and sexual morality which many strove earnestly to keep: and more succeeded than cynics would have us believe. Furthermore, some areas of life were regarded as the preserve of men or of women, not of both. Women did not have the vote in England, for example, until the early 1920s, and there was much resistance, not least from women, to their being given it. Even for women who, untypically, were determined on a career outside the home, many professions were closed. The public and grammar schools were universally single-sex, and there were far more academic schools for boys than for girls. Oxford and Cambridge, despite allowing women to attend lectures and tutorials, formally debarred them from degrees until very late: in Cambridge's case, until 1947. The Colleges of Oxford and Cambridge were all single-sex institutions, nearly all male. Women students had to be accompanied by a chaperone if their tutor was male and single: one reason why young Tolkien got many women pupils was that he was married, and their colleges did not have to provide chaperones. Even twenty years after 1945, a male Cambridge or Oxford don would expect to spend several evenings a week with colleagues and pupils in College discussing matters of common concern, while his wife looked after the children at home.

Though the world was changing, and some men and women were actively working for that change, many were happy enough with the status quo. There were good things in it: for example, the tender protectiveness towards women that could be, and was, developed in not a few men. These conventions, swept away for ever by the two World Wars, of course affected relationships. Friendships have to be based on common interest and knowledge, and this social situation encouraged single-sex friendship. Male friendship (often intense) was the norm, and was encouraged in all sorts of ways. The educated saw it as recapturing the ideal of Platonic friendship, where each Friend sought the other's ultimate good in the search for the True and the Beautiful; it was encouraged by popular books like *Tom Brown's Schooldays* and *Tom Brown at Oxford*, which had a considerable effect on the perception and expectation of both those environments by parents and adolescents. It was encouraged by social structures, making easy, unchaperoned contact between young men and women of the middle and upper classes rare. For Tolkien's generation and class, most of a man's most significant relationships would be with men. His friendships at all-male King Edward's were an important part of his intellectual development: boys (or girls) who have shared the wonder of feeling the air for the first time under their

14

intellectual wings do develop a very close relationship. In Oxford, similarly, his crucial intellectual relationships were with men of common interests and equal intelligence and learning. This does not necessarily imply misogyny, or homosexuality, or anything else of the kind. Rather, we are talking about the idea of Fellowship: the sort of mutual male dependence that is implied in the very title of the first volume of *LR*. Antony Powell's *A Question of Upbringing* (1951) gives a sharp view of the almost exclusively upper- and middle-class Oxford male society in the 1920s and 1930s; another, with strong hints of the homosexuality that undoubtedly did exist, is in Waugh's *Brideshead Revisited* (1945).

Oxford and Cambridge were – and are – peculiar places simply because of the high concentration of extremely intelligent people pursuing a variety of specialist interests. Before Oxford's development as an industrial centre (well under way by the 1930s) the University dominated the life of the town as it still did in Cambridge in the 1960s. The literary culture ranged from the serious to the playful and fantastic. The fiction of Lewis and Tolkien, like the detective stories of J. I. M. Stewart ('Michael Innes'), complemented, and were ultimately dependent on, their professional interests as scholars. Moreover, Oxford was a city of people of common interest endlessly getting together simply to talk. Tolkien was as clubbable as anyone, apparently; less typical in its subject, if typical in its formation, was his group, the Coalbiters. They met for no more and no less than the serious business of fun, and gathered round Tolkien and Lewis in 1929 to read the extant Old Norse sagas in the original ('Coalbiters' – those who sit over the fire, I suppose – translates the Icelandic *Kolbitar*). The sagas record heroic exploits, battles against great odds, vengefulness, crime; they also deal with the terrible predicaments of men and women trapped in webs of obligations that conflict, where every choice is wrong. (Tolkien's own story of Túrin Turambar owes a lot to the tragic saga of Grettir.) The *Voluspa* and the Elder *Edda*, moreover, record a cosmology and a theogony in which these ancient people – ancestors of the English – once believed: and like the humans, the gods too are caught in a net of fate, and the end will be the death of the gods in Ragnarök, the Last Battle, and the triumph of the Giants. Lewis and Tolkien were attracted by what Lewis called 'northernness', and Tolkien, when much younger, had read William Morris's versions of some of the sagas. (He was dismissive of Wagner's operatic treatment of the story of Fafnir, Siegfried, Brunnhilde, and the Götterdämmerung.) Reading the surviving literature of this culture must affect those who did it, and Tolkien's dwarves have names and habits straight from the sagas.

This sort of committed male fellowship is important in Tolkien's fiction, especially in *The Hobbit* and *LR*. A group of men becomes united, despite their individuality, in a common purpose, a common search; or, more pointedly, a group whose differences are no longer individual but specific – Dwarf, Elf, Men, Hobbits, Wizard – unites to fight the Enemy that threatens them all. This positively precludes the sort of role for and depiction of women with which other writers – Hardy, Lawrence, Joyce, Woolf, for example – had changed the world. Yet there are female characters in Tolkien's fiction which suggest a sympathy with their predicament, which, in another type of story, might have allowed him to put them centre stage with success.

And, of course, nobody is unaffected by what he reads. If you spend your days reading books and poems from a world where women are honoured, put on a pedestal – worshipped, even – where the chief male values are courage, and honesty, and honour, and generosity, you will in the end come to think in those terms (and may suffer no harm). Tolkien's intellectual diet from an early age had been just that: from George Macdonald's fantasies *The Princess and the Goblin* (1872) and *The Princess and Curdie* (1882), through stories collected in Andrew Lang's twelve *Fairy Books* to his version of the *Volsungasaga* and then, in maturity, to the riches of medieval and ancient literature, to the courts of Arthur and the halls of Asgard, to the tragedy of Deirdre and the sons of Usna and the love of Pwyll and Rhiannon. When Father Morgan extracted that promise not to contact Edith, there was no question, in his or her mind, but that it should be kept. The period of waiting, in which he passed through the years of greatest change in any man's life and might easily have transferred his affection elsewhere, seems, for Tolkien, to have been seen as almost a Romance test: he was obedient to the prohibition, the *geas*, laid on him, and proved his honour by his obedience, and by his faithfulness to Edith. The self-denial and the integrity of Aragorn and Arwen, of Beren and Lúthien, are rooted in the way a middle-class boy of conventional education and morality read about and loved stories written for a world long gone, stories which perhaps did not record the world as it was, but as it might or should be: and had his own conduct affected by them. 'Trouthe is the hyeste thing that man may kepe', says Chaucer's Arveragus: honour mattered. In France, young men really did go knowingly to their death because honour demanded it of them. In the early days, many echoed Rupert Brooke's 'Now God be thanked Who has matched us with His hour' (from 'Peace'), seeing the war as chivalric and noble, their cause a cause worth dying for. These are the values, unfashionable, perhaps inconceivable, now, held by many in Tolkien's generation, and by not a few in later ones. They are the values that lie at the heart of the fictions of Middle-earth.

2

The Critic

Tolkien had for years explored his invented languages and scripts as well as real ones. He found the months in 1919-20 working on the *New English Dictionary* (then at 'W') entirely to his taste. The *Dictionary*, 'On Historical Principles', demands for each word that different shades of meaning be distinguished and supported with attributed quotation from written sources, and that the family tree of that word, its cousins and relatives and ancestors in other languages, even extinct ones, be recorded. Tolkien said he learnt more about how languages worked then than in any other period of his career. The coherence of the tongues in *LR* is greatly dependent on that experience.

Such examination of words raises interesting problems. For example, are words merely sounds, to which by convention we attribute a given meaning, or do they in some way relate to the inner nature of things? Would the word 'wasp' – an entry Tolkien wrote – have any meaning if all wasps miraculously ceased to exist? Does the ancestor of 'wasp', Anglo-Saxon or Old Teutonic, mean anything when nobody now uses those languages? Is there any connection between the beauty (or otherwise) of the sound of words – to which Tolkien was sensitive – and the meaning? Do (or can) words communicate before they are understood, as Eliot (*Selected Essays*, 3rd edn., 1951, 238) could argue of poetry? Can one invent a new language that will not import into itself associations and ideas from the 'real world'? Are all languages governed by the same sort of rules? This is a Chomskyan position which Lewis anticipates: his character Ransom – whose philological expertise seems modelled on Tolkien's – in *Out of the Silent Planet* (1938, ch. 9), feels he might discover the 'very form of language itself, the principle behind all possible languages'.

Moreover, the connection between philology, the theory of

story, and anthropology has always been close. In the nineteenth century students of folk- and fairy-tale, *Märchen*, like the brothers Grimm, Jakob (1785–1863) and Wilhelm (1786–1859), who collected what they saw as 'primitive' narratives for scientific purposes, were also students of linguistics and the history of language. Jakob formulated in his *Deutsche Grammatik* (1819–37) the law of mutation of consonants in Aryan languages which is the foundation of modern historical linguistics. Andrew Lang (1844–1912), whose 'Fairy Books' were until recently given to many children, saw himself as an anthropologist, exploring the intimate relationship between folklore and developed mythology and religion. So these issues in the end address not only how we know, but the nature of that knowledge, and relate to concerns about the nature of story: for stories operate through language. These are questions of some relevance to the creator of a world with an articulated history, and with several different, developed languages. Indeed, Lewis and Tolkien argue that all stories are leaves on the same tree, that all lead us back to the trunk and the roots and the soil and the water that is the very ground of our existence. The corollary would follow that it is impossible to write a story that is *in essence* new, though it might be greatly inventive in the matter of its *accidents*. Some influential theorists have argued similarly: for example, Vladimir Propp, *Morphology of the Folk Tale* (1968).

These two concerns, with story and with language, are raised by the fourteenth-century English romance *Sir Gawain and the Green Knight*. The poem is of great linguistic interest, and it also contains narrative elements – the Beheading Game, the Exchange of Winnings, the Quest – which it is tempting to connect in some way with folklore and even, perhaps, long-forgotten cult practices. For a long time after the appearance of Tolkien's and Gordon's edition (1925), which was on most University English School reading lists for over forty years, it was possible to hear students talking glibly of the Green Knight as a 'Vegetation God' – a species few of them had met – and feeling that they were saying something important about *the poem*. But Tolkien's and Gordon's introduction sets out what they saw as the job of an editor of an old text: that is, not to dismember it into anthropological gobbets, or to provide a family tree for the descent of its various components, or to treat it as fodder for a dictionary, but, rather, 'to provide a sufficient apparatus for reading this *remarkable poem* with an appreciation as fast as possible *of the sort which its author may be supposed to have desired'* (p. v, italics mine). To that end, the glossary is very full, 'directed towards determining, as precisely as possible, the meaning of the author's actual words (in so far as the manuscript is fair to him)'. This asserts the importance of the poem as an artistic whole, and is a long way from later ideas of the 'Death of the Author', and from the ideas of the Intentional Fallacy which in 1946 W. K. Wimsatt, Jr. and Monroe C. Beardsley were to elaborate in their essay of that title, reprinted in Wimsatt's *The Verbal Icon* (1954). Tolkien's and Gordon's editorial stance presupposes authorial intention and artistic purpose that is *now* recoverable and operative in *our* reading of the poem. Moreover, the insistence on the poet's poem as a whole puts it centre stage and relegates that body of scholarship on 'the nature and significance of the "test"; the sources, near and remote, of the story's elements and details...and so on ...though not without interest', to the sidelines. This critical position Tolkien later developed in his *Beowulf* lecture, and it underlies his concept of his own work. In the Foreword to *Farmer Giles of Ham* (1949) he parodies the stance and tone of the editorial procedure which he and Gordon attacked, and lets the subsequent narrative subvert that parodic voice; and in the first edition of *LR*, he again poses as the objective editor of a transmitted text. (Even in the 1966 second edition, where he acknowledges the fiction of *LR* and talks of its development, there is still some hedging: as if active, 'the tale grew in the telling', p. 5). More to the immediate point, the assertion of a recoverable authorial intention, a meaning, chimes exactly with the ideas Tolkien developed, and with an orthodox (even old-fashioned) Christian understanding of the way the Mind of God may be read in his creation – the world that Boccaccio in the fourteenth century called 'God's poem'. The authority of St Paul (*Romans*, 1: 19–20) and of the Augustinian idea of God revealing himself in the two Books of Scripture and of Nature, underlie this attitude.

Since the work of Saussure, Althusser, de Man, and Barthes, modern critical perspectives have more or less consistently stressed the act of reading a text as the focus of interest. The author's intentions are unknowable: all the reader can rely on is the text, which, examined from a number of standpoints, can reveal its internal incoherences and *aporie*, its socio-economic assumptions, and topics that it tacitly admits its inability to address. Of course, the reader's reaction, on these terms, is itself merely provisional, and open to the same sort of deconstruction as the victim text. (Tolkien's and Gordon's statement of their critical principles is also open to this challenge, of course.) Furthermore, the extreme scepticism of philosophers and critics like Derrida denies the possibility of any coherent, or determinate, meaning in language, and subverts the whole of the Western philosophic tradition which relies on exactly the assumption of the possibility of such meaning. Now it is certain that Tolkien, and Lewis, and others of their circle would have had little time for such theoretical standpoints, even though, active as scholars and teachers until well into the 1960s, they cannot have been unaware of some structuralist ideas. (An Oxford or Cambridge College High Table is a very good place for learning about the latest intellectual excitement in any field.) Their rejection, discernible in their fictional practice and their later critical writings, is not, however, merely a gruff refusal to contemplate such thoughts: rather, it grows out of a fundamentally Platonic view of language and knowledge. In a word, language and knowledge *are* unstable, provisional, constantly needing revision: but this shadowy knowledge, this indistinct speech, is communicating something of great pith and moment, just as the Shadows on the wall of Plato's Cave (*Republic*, vii) are not real, but indicate the existence, and the partial knowability, of real Things.

The poem *Mythopoeia* marks an important stage in the articulation of this transcendental view of *poiesis*. Its title means 'a making of fables' – a sense going back to Diodorus Siculus and Plutarch – but also puns on 'speaking through myth'. Subtitled 'Philomythus to Misomythus' ('a lover of myth to a hater of myth'), it originated as a reply to Lewis, after that crucial talk, recorded in Lewis's *Surprised by Joy*, on 19 September 1931 between Tolkien, Lewis, and Dyson, when Dyson and Tolkien propounded to Lewis, then not a Christian, the 'true myth' of Christ. The poem's importance is its clue to the drift of Tolkien's mind in the early 1930s, when the myths of *The Silmarillion* were well-developed, but long before *LR* was conceived. (The poem went through seven versions before publication in 1988.) *Mythopoeia* insists, first, on a theistic view of Nature, already common ground between Tolkien and Lewis. Language, through a 'faint echo and dim picture of the world', allows Man to grasp the world he inhabits, to '[dig] the foreknown from experience, | and [pan] the vein of spirit out of sense'. Moreover, Man, though 'estranged' from the 'only Wise', is 'not wholly lost', 'draws some wisdom', and is

> subcreator, the reflected light
> through whom is splintered from a single White
> to many hues, and endlessly combined
> in living shapes that move from mind to mind.

From this, the poem asserts Man's necessity to create and imagine, and that the charge against fantasy and myth and transcendent ideas of beauty of 'wish fulfilment' misses the point:

> Whence came the wish, and whence the power to dream,
> Or some things fair and others ugly deem?

In other words, did the Good and the Beautiful not exist independently, we could not know things were good and beautiful. (T. S. Eliot comes close to a similar position in the last chorus from *The Rock* (1934), and in 'Burnt Norton' (1936)). The climax of the poem insists on the *moral* duty of man to assert the existence of the good and the true, to seek truth through myth, to exercise his God-given function of subcreation,

> I bow not yet before the Iron Crown,
> Nor cast my own small golden sceptre down.

These lines are particularly revealing, for Tolkien is using his own imagined world of *The Silmarillion*, parts of which had been read to Lewis, as a reference-point for action and understanding in this one: the lines are meaningless unless we know the Satanic figure of Morgoth and his Iron Crown. The close of the poem depends heavily on the imagery of the *Revelation of St John the Divine*: another mythopoeic text. This poem shows how important discussion among The Inklings was to the elaboration of their ideas about story and the nature of imaginative writing. Each contributed to the others' thoughts and theories, and the fiction of Lewis, Williams, and Tolkien shares many assumptions about what Tolkien called 'sub-creation'. So some of Lewis's essays on these topics can illuminate the practice of Tolkien and Williams as well as his own: several use the fictions of Williams and Tolkien as supporting evidence.

Lewis's essay 'On Stories' (1947) asserts that modern critics tend to ignore story, the series of imagined events, as against other things like style and character. But he recalls Aristotle's theory of fiction which makes story ('plot', *mythos*), more important than character; the fourteenth-century demonstration by Boccaccio of the value of reading the *narrative* of pagan mythologies allegorically; and, finally, Jung's idea of Archetypes in myth, legend, and literature, which all new narrative elements reflect. This stress on the importance of story connects with his theory of the nature of an audience's pleasure. Why do we re-read when we know 'what happens'? Lewis suggests that the reader 'is not looking for surprises, but a certain surprisingness' (p. 17). We may have a delight in 'otherness' of the strange, the unquantifiable; we may have a perception of pattern, and sometimes the imagining of what we know not to be real may be the only way of approaching crucial moral and intellectual questions. As an example, Lewis cites how many stories turn on the fulfilling of prophecies, and how steps taken to prevent the fulfilment actually bring it about. The prime example is the story of Oedipus, and the reader's perception of pattern and awareness of irony presents in a way the imagination can grasp what has 'always baffled the intellect – we have *seen* how destiny and free will can be combined, even how free will is the *modus operandi* of destiny' (p. 15). Thus 'one of the functions of art is to present what the narrow and desperately practical perspectives of real life exclude' (p. 10). In other words, art offers possibilities and perspectives, and an 'excursion into the preposterous [which] sends us back with renewed pleasure to the real.... Something which the educated receive from poetry can reach the masses through stories of adventure, and almost in no other way' (p. 16). Precisely this sort of understanding of plot lies behind the narratives of *LR* and *The Silmarillion*.

The paper 'On Three Ways of Writing for Children' (1952) was written after the success of the early stories of Narnia, Lewis's own imagined universe. Lewis clearly supports Tolkien's diagnosis in 'On Fairy Stories' that the appeal of the 'fairy story' lies in man there most fully exercising his function as a sub-creator, making not a 'comment upon life' but his own subordinate world. In Lewis's and Tolkien's view, Man is endowed by the God who created him with the responsibility himself to create: this is one of Man's proper – God-given – functions, and delight arises when we see it successfully done. Furthermore, as fairy-tale draws on the Archetypes in the collective unconscious, when we read a good tale we *recognize*, but in a new way, what we knew already. Moreover, in common experience, fiction can give us a pattern on which to interpret real new experience, to which we match it. Lewis made this point in his autobiography, *Surprised by Joy* (1955), when, soaked in Homer, he first finds himself in the trenches in 1918 and hears the shells screaming overhead: 'this is war. This is what Homer wrote about' (ch. 12). The archetype – and the way to cope with it – surfaced out of the deep past.

Often, for both of them, this experience was accompanied by *Sehnsucht* – in Lewis's words, a 'longing for he knows not what': as the Tookish part of Bilbo feels, indeed. A reader is 'stir[red] ... with a dim sense of something beyond his reach and ... gives the actual world a new dimension of depth'. Lewis chose the opening words of one of Wordsworth's most profound sonnets as the title for his autobiography to remind us of the discussion of this sense of joy, and loss, and being on the brink of knowledge, which is at the heart of Wordsworth's exploration of the growth of a poet's mind.

Tolkien articulated his theory of art and sub-creation and its philosophical importance most fully in 1936–9. These years seem crucial in his developing understanding of himself as a writer, as they are the key years for his writing itself. The Andrew Lang lecture, 'On Fairy Stories', given in the University of St Andrews on 8 March, 1939 is his fullest statement. Tolkien said that 'Leaf by Niggle', which with clear Christian symbolism exemplifies the ideas of the essay, belonged with it, written 'when *LR* was beginning to unroll itself' – that is, a few months after the publication of *The Hobbit*, and a year or so after the delivery to the British Academy, on 25 November, 1936, of the lecture 'Beowulf: The Monsters and the Critics'.

The *Beowulf* lecture grew from teaching poems separated from us not only by a dead language, but also by their origin in an unknowable mind set in a long-dead culture. Questions arise about what a highly intelligent and sophisticated poet, in whose England dragons and monsters like Grendel were observably uncommon, thought he was doing, and what his audience thought they were listening to: and how we, the audience he could never have envisaged, might respond to the poem. Consistent with the ideas in 'Mythopoeia', the lecture is essentially a defence of *poiesis*, and reclaims *Beowulf* as an artistic whole against a piecemeal approach to it as a jumble of literary *topoi* – exactly the approach in the edition of *Gawain*. The majority of those who had hitherto discussed the poem tended to explore aspects of philological, archaeological, anthropological, or historical interest alone. Such critics Tolkien wittily casts as monsters, like Grendel, who would bite its head off or tear it into little pieces to see what it was made of. Tolkien's persuasion of his audience, indeed, depends heavily on the metaphor and allegory his opponents' methodology must ignore. He gives the analogy of the poem as a tower ('Monsters and Critics', pp. 248–9) built of stones from a former building, erected to give a view of the distant sea. The monsters, the critics, want to demolish that tower to look at the stones, and will not look at the vision that takes the breath. They forget that the poem is a haunting, moral study of a *man*, Beowulf, rising through his valour to a pinnacle of earthly glory and then inevitably falling from it. When young, he aids Hrothgar against Grendel, and makes himself worthy of the kingship he at first declines; as an old king he thinks to aid his people by fighting the dragon, and is destroyed. All earthly glory is merely an interim: Beowulf's kingdom will now be vulnerable to the Swedes.

> The significance of a myth is not easily to be pinned on paper by analytical reasoning [which is all the critics and philologists have to use]. It is at its best when it is presented by a poet who *feels rather than makes explicit* what his theme portends; who presents it *incarnate in the world of history and geography*, as our poet has done. ('Monsters and Critics', pp. 256–7; my itals.)

This reflects interestingly on Tolkien's assumptions about the world he himself was creating. A serious critical position is being advanced; but it is also hard not to hear Tolkien talking as the author of *The Hobbit* as well as philologist or critic.

The first section of 'On Fairy Stories' defines what fairy story is, and attacks Lang for the same faults as those monstrous critics, approaching his collections as a folklorist or anthropologist, misunderstanding the nature and purpose of fairy-stories so that he includes things – like beast-fable – which can by no means so be classed ('Fairy Stories', p. 18). Second, Tolkien discusses how fairy-stories begin, suggesting that they grow from the accumulated 'stew' of centuries of myth and story and history, what he calls the 'Pot' of story, and touch deep levels of our subconscious as human beings; how events in a story may reverberate in our minds because they relate to or echo remembered paradigms which may be parabolic utterances of the way the world is. He discusses Fantasy, the ability (and need) of human beings to escape imaginatively from 'the domination of observed "fact"' ('Fairy Stories', p. 45), and to create a secondary world where strange, arresting things not in our primary world can have a credible existence. This is essentially an art that can *only* be performed by literature, for the visual arts limit into definiteness that which words can suggest. Words solicit our cooperation in creation; picture (and drama) our assent. Though fantasy, the creation of subsidiary worlds, can be horribly misused, it remains a basic human instinct and a right: abuse of a thing does not take away its inherent utility. 'We make in our measure and in our derivative mode, because we are made: and not only made, but made in the image and likeness of a Maker' ('Fairy Stories', p. 52).

Here is the heart of Tolkien's thinking. God has deputed to his creature the ability to create. It is this that validates his subcreation – and gives a standard of value by which to judge it. The next section of the essay, 'Recovery, Escape, Consolation', maintains that through fairy-story, and through art, we recover the sense of the wonder of the familiar; we can alter our perspective to see the magic of the everyday, the mystery of (as Hopkins put it) 'all trades, their gear and tackle and trim'. 'Creative fantasy' may transfigure the familiar. But the heart of this section lies in rebutting the charge of 'escapism' levelled at fantasy, at art, at the consolations of religion. (It was to be levelled dismissively at Tolkien's own stories.) Tolkien's strategy is, quite simply, to accept the word, and to argue that to desire to escape is the rational and proper desire of the captive. The magical world of Faerie satisfies very deep human desires – above all, the desire for escape from the limitations of mortal life and from Death itself. (*Beowulf*, which must be seen as tragic or at least elegiac, offers no such vision: there man is overwhelmed by chaos and death.) Tolkien suggests that the fairy-story can prompt feelings of wonder, of joy, of desire for we know not what, of eucatastrophe – the rightness of the unexpected, uncovenanted 'happy ending' in those who retain something of the vision of the Wordsworthian child of the *Immortality Ode*, who resist the closing of the walls of the prison house about them. (He stresses that fantasy is as important to adults as to children, and that he himself only came to enjoy fairy-stories *as he matured*.) In this sub-created world, we glimpse a Joy 'beyond the walls of the world, poignant as grief' that illuminates and transfigures the suffering that we know, and without which that Joy would be meaningless.

Tolkien writes as a Christian. As an educated one, he is perfectly aware of narrative elements in the Gospel which have analogues in other myths and other cultures. But rather than seeing this as detracting from the possibility of the story being true, he thinks the opposite: that myth, and structures of narrative, may resurface time and again in fairy-story simply because they are *essentially* true, grounded in a greater Truth of which they are shadows. Both he and Lewis claim that the 'fairy-story' ('Fairy Stories', p. 65) of the Gospels is 'of a larger kind which embraces all the essence of fairy stories...among the marvels is the greatest and most complete conceivable eucatastrophe. But this story has entered History and the primary world: the desire and aspiration of sub-creation has been raised to the fulfilment of Creation.'

This is not simply a polemical position: Tolkien really believed it, as the moving letter to his son Christopher in November 1944 (*Letters*, pp. 99ff.) makes clear. So thoroughgoing a Christian theory of art has not been so fully articulated, from a position of unusual learning and from direct experience of creative composition, this century. Its claims for the authority of the maker (to use a Middle English word for a poet) would not find many echoes in academic circles in the last few decades; its claims about the nature of fable, its claims about the possibility of Truth and that language can convey determinate meaning would get short shrift from most contemporary orthodoxies. But it is entirely consistent with a major strand in European philosophy of literature stretching back through, for example, Wordsworth, Coleridge, and Milton to the fourteenth century and beyond.

The word 'Platonic' was used above of Tolkien's theory of *poiesis*. That Platonic cast underlies many earlier theories of art. For Dante (*Convivio*, ii), fiction was the beautiful lie draped over Truth, which attracted us to knowledge: poetry teaches a truth through a fiction, a shadow of truth. For Boccaccio (*De Genealogia Deorum*, xiv, esp. 7, 8, 12, and xv), fable (*fabula*) was many-layered, yielding to the perceptive mind and the inquiring intellect many truths, even truth hidden from the original authors. For Petrarch (*Invectives*, iii), the poet's inspiration by the Muses is a God-given gift, comparable to the work of the Holy Spirit. Torquato Tasso (*Discorsi del Poema Eroico*, 1594) explores the idea of the poet as sub-creator imitating God's world. In England a few years earlier Sir Philip Sidney brilliantly synthesized the ideas of Horace, Cicero, Aristotle, and Plato about poetry – that is, the art of fiction – and why it is important. He stresses how important is the pleasure the poet gives 'with a tale, which holdeth children from play, and old men from the Chimney corner', for it can have a profound moral effect in giving a 'sweet prospect' into the path of virtue. But he also suggests the sort of view Tolkien explored:

> Onely the Poet...lifted up with the vigour of his own invention, doth grow in effect into an other nature: in making things either better then nature bringeth foorth, or, quite a newe, formes such as never were in Nature: as the *Heroes, Demigods, Cyclops, Chymeras, Furies,* and such like; so as hee goeth hand in hand with nature, not enclosed within the narrow warrant of her gifts, but freely raunging within the Zodiack of his owne wit. Nature never set foorth the earth in so rich Tapistry as diuers Poets have done, neither with so plesaunt rivers, fruitfull trees, sweete smelling flowers, nor whatsoeuer els may make the too much loved earth more lovely: her world is brasen, the Poets onely deliver a golden. (*Defence of Poesie*, 8)

> ...Give right honor to the heavenly maker of that maker [the poet], who having made man to his owne likenes, set him beyond and over

28

all the workes of that second nature, which in nothing he sheweth so much as in Poetry; when with the force of a divine breath, he bringeth things foorth surpassing her doings...our erected wit maketh us know what perfectiō is, and yet our infected wit keepeth us frō reaching unto it. (pp. 8–9)

This is as near as makes no matter Tolkien's view: see, for example, p. 52 of 'On Fairy Stories'. But with him there is that addition that in the end, all stories are parts of One Story. C. S. Lewis, in another context, put it succinctly: 'one's mind runs up the sunbeam to the Sun'.

3

A World of Words

The stories of Middle-earth are really one book, and writing it took Tolkien all his life: and unawares. Despite much polishing after writing, he seems not to have planned, so much as discovered, what he has to say. *The Hobbit* grew from a single sentence, and he had apparently no idea what a hobbit was or how to finish the book. Similarly with *LR*: the introductory note to *Tree and Leaf* (1964–5) describes

> when the *LR* was beginning to unroll itself and to unfold prospects of labour and exploration in yet unknown country as daunting to me as to the hobbits. At about that time we had reached Bree, and I had then no more notion that they had of what had become of Gandalf, or who Strider was; and I had begun to despair of finding out. (Cf. Foreword to 2nd edn. of *LR*, 1966, 5)

The story itself is cast as active, the writer as passive. Suggesting himself as a heroic hobbit on a quest, with companions ('we'), could be disingenuous, a conceit which orders untidy experience and implies the story as somehow independent of its redactor. (Later he was to authorize his own fiction by posing, in its preliminaries and appendices, as merely its editor – a further fiction.) But this suspicion need not destroy the essential honesty of Tolkien's consistent description of how he wrote. For what starts as an apparently trivial children's story, faltering in tone and clumsy in writing, does seem unpremeditatedly to collide with the world of *The Silmarillion* about half-way through, and the seriousness with which Tolkien was taking his story seems to rise with the rhetorical level (one might recall Lewis's remarks in 'On Stories', 39). Much in Tolkien's letters supports the *Tree and Leaf* account of the composition of *LR*. Moreover, he kept recasting earlier material in version after elaborated version. So there is more than a grain of truth in presenting himself as an editor: he is indeed editing and reinterpreting the work of another man, that self he was when first he created those stories.

His sources – if 'sources' is the word – are only the stones that form the tower: Tolkien's warning should be heeded. But they range interestingly widely. Early reading of, for example, George Macdonald's *The Princess and the Goblin*, and *The Princess and Curdie* echoes in the episode in the Misty Mountains in *The Hobbit*. Barrie's *Peter Pan* (1904 and 1911) he loved; he admired Francis Thompson's verse, especially 'Sister Songs' (1895), where elves dance in the greenwood as they do in Tolkien's early verse. Galadriel in *LR* has a hint of Rider Haggard's Ayesha in *She* (1887); and the structure of a band of adventurers travelling into the unknown is much the pattern of Haggard's fiction, together with all that *Boys' Own Paper* school of writers who hitched their bandwagon to that popular star. Things in the Dead Marshes recall Sedgmoor in Blackmore's *Lorna Doone* (1871, ii, pp. 290 ff.). Kenneth Grahame's Mole and Ratty in *The Wind in the Willows* (1908) are among Bilbo's ancestors, not least in the delight in a good table (though we rarely get details of what was on it). Tolkien's tour in the Alps gave the detail in Bilbo's journey through the Misty Mountains of the rocks falling from the high ice over the path. Merry's sword from the Barrow Downs, which dislimns when it pierces the Lord of the Nazgûl, recalls the ancient sword which dissolves when Beowulf slays Grendel's mother; while Bilbo taking the cup from Smaug's treasure recalls Wiglaf's action in *Beowulf*. The name 'orc' is Anglo-Saxon for 'goblin' (which raises another problem, of course). Rohan recreates a heroic Anglo-Saxon society; and the siege of Gondor, with details like the enemy catapulting the heads of fallen friends into the city, owes something to descriptions of the taking of Constantinople by Mehmet II in 1453. The downfall of Númenor recalls Plato's story of Atlantis in *The Republic*. Aragorn and Gandalf recall Arthur and Merlin (although it is more Tennyson's Arthur than Malory's). The Elves of *LR* are medieval romance figures, courtly, musical, polished, at home in the greenwood, powerful and potentially dangerous – like the faery folk that stole Tam Lin away. But these noble creatures are also related to the 'Elvish knights' of Spenser's *The Faerie Queene*. The

Dwarves are Old Norse in their names, their feuds, their revenges: and the Petty Dwarf Mîm in *The Silmarillion* resembles Mime in the *Nibelungenlied*. The incest motif from that poem reappears in the terrible fate of Túrin and Niniel in *The Silmarillion*; and in the saga of Grettir the Strong Túrin Turambar's tragic fate is anticipated. Indeed, nineteenth-century philological research into the Germanic tongues, giving startling glimpses of hitherto unknown ages, provided a major impulse and imaginative space for writers of extended fantasies, such as William Morris. Tolkien and Morris, for example, discovered in Old Norse Eddic poetry the same Mirkwood the Great, and each used it in a new fictional setting. Verbally, some names may recall the pleasure of the mere sound remembered from a book: Beleriand may echo the name 'Belerion' which Diodorus Siculus gave Cornwall, the regal syllables of Númenor suggest the Latin *numen*, 'power, divine majesty': and 'Sauron' suggests both Satan and something reptilian. The name Eärendil (its latest form) comes from the haunting lines of Cynewulf, 'Eala Earendel engla beorhtast | ofer middangeard monnum sended' – 'Earendel, brightest of the angels sent over earth to men' (*Advent*, ll. 104–5). Carpenter, p. 72, records Tolkien saying that on reading those lines 'something had stirred in me, half wakened from sleep.' But these details are cosmetic rather than structural. It is the mythic nature of the quest underlying many stories, the mythic nature of many legends where other species, even trees, talk, that matter more than Tolkien's specific reading of Grahame or Haggard or Spenser or *Beowulf*. His ideas of the 'pot' of story in 'On Fairy Stories' are relevant – all these things simmering away in his mind for years. His own analogy, years later, of *LR* 'growing like a seed in the dark out of the leaf mould of the mind' put it well: the leaves in that mould are those from the Tree.

Tolkien's fiction is difficult to categorize. Allen and Unwin were so uncertain of what they had on their hands with *LR*, and at what market to aim it, that rather than write the usual publisher's blurb they sought recommendations from Naomi Mitchison, Richard Hughes, and C. S. Lewis. (Lewis invoked as comparisons science fiction, Spenser, Malory, and Ariosto, and attracted a lot of criticism from reviewers for so doing. He also reviewed it in *Time and Tide,* and had already reviewed *The Hobbit,* anonymously, in *The Times* in September 1937.) That confusion about what the book was echoes in the reviews; it is easily forgotten how taxonomy affects judgement of a new work. The same sort of critical tools cannot be used to discuss a play as one would a novel, or a romance as one would a *roman policier.* It may be useful, therefore, to glance at some of the generic links of Tolkien's work and at some of the things it is not.

The Lord of the Rings ignores the whole development of the novel as the most resourceful, and central, verbal fictional form from Conrad through Joyce and Kafka and Woolf, from Hardy through Lawrence. It ignores the extraordinary strengths of that form in the delicate exploration of the self, drawing on the work of Freud and his successors. It does not even ground itself in the realist conventions of the nineteenth-century novel. It is not a *Bildungsroman;* it is certainly not a novel of manners. Its nearest analogues within the genre are perhaps the Gothic novel – such as Maturin's *Melmoth the Wanderer* (1820) – and the historical narratives of Walter Scott. There is more than a *soupçon* of the 'adventure story' of Stevenson and other, lesser, writers. It is, in effect, literally *sui generis,* and before its appearance there is only one modern book in any way comparable with it, E. R. Eddison's *The Worm Ouroboros* (1926). That also deals with an unending struggle against dark forces in an imagined world, with its own language, its own mythology: Lewis thought well of it. But long before 1926 Tolkien had developed the mythology behind *LR.* In fact, the nearest parallels to Tolkien's work lie in medieval romance, in the Irish *imram* or journey narrative, in saga, in epic: those genres formed his critical criteria, and inform his own fiction.

The category 'fantasy' is common enough in bookshops and publishers' catalogues, and is often where Tolkien and his literary descendants are to be located. But the term's precise definition is still problematical, and its discussion does not yet have an agreed critical methodology. This is one reason why Tolkien's discussion of the Fairy Story can be helpful. (One might prefer to 'Fairy' the Spenserian spelling 'Faerie', so as not to forget that the 'parallel world' can be as cruel and dangerous as our own, not a place of pretty children with butterfly wings.) Put together with Lewis's 'On Stories' and 'On Three Ways of

Writing for Children', it might suggest a basis for discussion. For example: 'Story'– perhaps Aristotle's term *mythos* might be better – is paramount; events have a shape and a meaning which drives the whole thing along. The story is moral; it will draw on ancient motifs and paradigms. It will cleanse our vision of this world, and help us to order our priorities. It will generate that unsuspected, not-to-be-satisfied desire which values other satisfiable desires. And, like all good fiction, it will alter our reality.

Whether medieval or modern, nobody expects fantasy/ romance to operate in a material world like ours. Its world is freed of those limitations that we feel most constricting. Monsters stalk among its leaves as of right. Giants and dragons and magic springs are part of its natural history, and swords do get stuck in stones and helmets can be crafted by dwarves to give invisibility. It can bend reality as we might wish it bent. (It is certain Ents do not exist. But of all Tolkien's creations, this is perhaps the one we most wish did.) Faerie stories are not concerned with states of mind or development of character, as A. S. Byatt has pointed out in one of her own: some issues are simply not important. One might, in another sort of story cast in our world, properly ask about the economy of the Shire. Was it all only tobacco-growing in the south and mixed farming – mainly mushrooms – in the east? Where did the house of Elrond get its supplies of food? Then these issues must have obtruded, and weakened the credit we could give to characters and their actions. But precisely because this not our world, we accept it: just as the world of Chrétien de Troyes, as Auerbach pointed out (*Mimesis*, ch. 6, pp. 131 ff.), is at once unrealistic in its picture of society and utterly realistic in depicting what many people in that society cared about: courage, ethics, *gentilesse*. The moral/ethical challenge and analysis in the best romance, medieval or later, is as urgent as in any other good fiction. It is perfectly capable of tackling big political and religious issues, and topical ones at that – as do, for example, Wace's *Brut*, or Spenser's *Faerie Queene*.

The Silmarillion, as it eventually became, was started about 1917. The central narratives – for example, Beren's quest to wrest a Silmaril from Morgoth's Iron Crown as bride-price for Thingol's daughter – were in existence early, and were reworked in many different forms. Already the motif to which Tolkien often returned, the Quest journey through a Waste Land, the challenge to a Dark Tower – a challenge that in turn tests the maturity and integrity of the challenger – is dominant. The echoes of medieval Arthurian romance are patent, just as they are in T. S. Eliot's *The Waste Land* (1922); and both writers share an interest in the way the mythic stirs half-understood resonances in a reader's mind. These early narratives generate details which themselves demanded explanation, which could only be given by yet another narrative – and so on, back to the first Creation stories of the universe that Tolkien's imagination was bringing into being. It was sixty years before Tolkien's son published a version of *The Silmarillion*; and, as he remarked in his introduction, many of the stories were literally old, 'not only in their derivation from the remote First Age, but also in terms of my father's life'. Over the years, they had come to hold great significance for Tolkien, a mythology expressing his deepest concerns and values. Indeed, Jung's remarks on myth in *Memories, Dreams and Reflections* are relevant. Jung saw myth as an appropriate form of personal expression, because it is more individual and expresses life more precisely than does science. Of the truth of stories told as part of a personal myth, Jung remarks, 'whether or not the stories are "true" is not the problem. The only question is whether what I tell is *my* fable, *my* truth'. On Tolkien's mythology his entire fictional output depends.

The Silmarillion has only the loosest of unities. Though the narratives are put in a chronological sequence, Tolkien's mind did not work so. Often the 'earlier' story – in point of time in the invented universe – was written to explain one already composed. The discrete narratives cross and recross each other's path: for example in chapter 23 Tuor and Voronwë pass the Pools of Irvin and see far off, 'going northward in haste . . . a tall Man, clad in black, and bearing a black sword'. They do not know that this is Turin, going to his terrible doom, which we have *already* seen: and they too are travelling to the doom of Gondolin (the first story Tolkien put on paper). Tolkien seems to be using a concept of narrative more familiar from very ancient stories than from anything to which the novel has accustomed us. Analogies, not absolutely exact, that spring to mind are with Homeric 'ring composition', in which the poet suspends the main narrative while the story of a man's youth, or a captive's history, or that of a piece of treasure, is brought right into the foreground and related in full. Another is with the complexity of interwoven narratives working round a single theme in Norse sagas. Another is with *entrelace* in the medieval romance, where co-ordinate stories weave together in a complex web: a sophisticated, subtle way of presenting a picture of the world we live in, where everyone is the hero of their own story. Perhaps the best analogy is with the detailed family trees Tolkien constructed for his characters, where relationships have an interconnected complexity that underscores the importance of everything and everyone to the whole.

Moreover, if a present narrative implies a past, it also implies a future. In Tolkien's major fiction, action in the present is of crucial consequence for the future, and he is always concerned to place a narrative in a historical continuum of other stories – even the independent *Farmer Giles* is located by its introduction in a fanciful, supposedly authentic, history relating to the reader's present. In *LR*, with a perspective reaching back over millennia, Tolkien subtly reminds us that this crisis is both conclusion and beginning, for, at the Council of Elrond, it is noticeable that the Company that eventually sets out not only represents the different peoples, but also (except for Gandalf), all are heirs: Legolas is heir of Thranduil, Gimli of Glóin, Strider of Isildur, Boromir of Denethor. And Frodo is Bilbo's, as Merry and Pippin are heirs of the other major branches of the hobbits, Buckland and Tookland. The young are saviour-figures of the old: and they must bear the weight of the suffering of the past. Moreover, the War of the Ring is both end of the Third Age and beginning of the Fourth, when the Elves will pass away. In such an aesthetic, final closure of the narrative is impossible: there can never be an 'ever after'. (It is precisely for that reason that Tolkien's narrative is framed by 'editorial' appendices and introductions which assert both the connectedness to an unnarrated corpus and the completedness of this particular text.)

The disciplines of philology were influential in this idea of literary form. By its nature, philological inquiry works backwards: the search for the history, and the prehistory, behind the contemporary word. In the Foreword to the second edition of *LR*, Tolkien says:

I had little hope that other people would be interested in this work [the mythology and philology of the Elder days, which he worked on after completing *The Hobbit*] especially since *it was primarily linguistic in inspiration.... was begun in order to provide the necessary background of 'history' for Elvish tongues...* the story was drawn irresistibly towards the older world. (p. 5, italics mine)

In effect, the narratives are a variant of the rhetorical device of *hysteron proton*, telling the later thing first: for example, Vergil tells us about Aeneas arriving in Libya before we know why he is at sea in the first place, and Conrad moves backwards in Marlow's life from *Heart of Darkness* to *Youth*. *The Hobbit* came from nowhere: as it grew, motifs like the finding of the ring, or the elves, or the destruction of Dale, came into the narrative. These implied a *pre*-narrative, not accommodatable in the immediate story; and as the world they were in was an imagined one, they were not common knowledge for the reader. The place whence the dragon, and the elves, and the history of the dwarves drew their being was, naturally, *The Silmarillion*, still unpublished – unpublishable then, indeed. But who were the Hobbits? Where did they come from? Who was Gollum? How did he come to have the Ring? These had no explanation. So *LR*, building on history and legend in *The Silmarillion*, begins its existence, in Stanley Unwin's intent, as 'the New *Hobbit*', as a sequel; but as it developed it became both a chronological sequel and, in the narratives of explanation from one character to another embedded within it and in its appendices, a predecessor to *The Hobbit*. In writing *LR*, Tolkien makes the crucial connection, or link, or amalgam, between the comfortable old-clothes world of *The Hobbit* and the high heroic *Silmarillion*. And this highlights a major theme of his writing: little people matter in the affairs of the great, and weakness, apparent foolishness, can be stronger than mere power. After *LR*, it is no longer possible to read *The Hobbit* as a naïf story. One is too aware of ironies and significances – almost Ian Watt's idea of 'delayed decoding' – of which characters (and the narratorial voice) are ignorant. The earlier book has been repositioned by the later; and when *The Silmarillion* was published, the reading of the *mythos* of *LR* was similarly altered.

The Lord of the Rings, Tolkien's most complex and ambiguous work, is the one that won his extraordinary readership. (Some admirers could not finish *The Silmarillion*.) The title's very cadence announces something more serious than its predecessor: *The Hobbit, or, There and Back Again* reassures with a child's joke – 'Where are you going?' 'Oh, there and back again.' *The Lord of the Rings'* narrative is overtly ambitious, with six 'books' recalling the customary divisions of an epic poem. Book I builds up the main theme of the Ring Quest, and the deepening awareness that fellowship, selflessness, and trust are all that can stand against relentless evil: and that there is often no choice as to whether or not we take part in the struggle, only on which side we shall be. Book II continues this thematic development, and the perspective of the narrative is deepened by the retrospective material revealed at the Council of Elrond and the journey through a landscape of legend, to the breaking of the Fellowship. The climax of Book II is the struggle in Boromir between fidelity to the bond of the Fellowship and what seems like sheer sense: the temptation to take, for the best motives, the Ring from Frodo. In III and IV, the company, now divided, becomes entangled with a huge complex of forces as the whole world goes to war: Merry and Pippin, Aragorn, Legolas, and Gimli with the Rohirrim and the struggle against Saruman; Frodo and Sam with the Dark Journey through the marshes, Ithilien, and into Mordor. Book III closes with Pippin revealing himself to Sauron through the Palantir, which precipitates the attack on Gondor; Book IV, in balance, closes with Frodo captured by Sauron's Orcs. All through Book V we hear nothing of Frodo, on whom the outcome of all the events ultimately rests. It is full of bustle as Rohan rides to Gondor, and the great battle is fought in the Pelennor Fields which repulses, for the time being, the forces of Sauron. The first part of Book VI completes, by a final ironic twist, Frodo's quest and Gollum's destiny, the utter rout of the forces of Mordor, and the aftermath of the struggle, concluding with the journey to a distant home that, not unchanged, has also been soiled by the struggle between good and evil. Continually, and increasingly climactically, Tolkien punctuates the romance motif of the troublous journey through a wild landscape of danger and trial with episodes at a place of sanctuary, whence departure to greater testing must soon follow: the Shire to the Old Forest, and then to Tom Bombadil's timeless house, where an unfallen Adam, Lord over his Garden, is as free from fear as from tyrannical intent; then the terrible journey to the Ford, and to the refuge of Elrond, a place that links the narrative back to the wars against Morgoth and his servants that lie in the prehistory of this narrative. From Rivendell, the journey through Moria, and the loss of Gandalf, to lovely Lothlórien, an unfallen earthly Paradise, protected by its queen Galadriel, as *The Silmarillion*'s Doriath was by its queen Melian. After Lothlórien, the journey in which the Fellowship is broken, and Boromir is lost. Even then, one side of the company finds precarious welcome in threatened Rohan or Gondor, the other unexpected, temporary solace with Faramir in Ithilien. Each refuge is less and less secure, more and more under threat: and from the last all go out to the final showdown.

The complexity of this structure is a development of the two-part structure of *The Hobbit*, where the journey and meeting the merely monstrous Gollum – whom one critic has called 'an autistic troglodyte' – dominate chapters 1–8, and the struggle with Smaug chapters 9–19. The binary pattern of journey/refuge running through the earlier book has been greatly developed, and extends to influence the structuring of characters and the symbolic opposition of place to place – Minas Tirith to Minas Morgul, Rivendell to Isengard, and so on: a structural opposition that recalls the Augustinian concept of the Two Cities. The plot-shape of *The Hobbit* is simple, closed: Bilbo returns rich to Bag End, and the story ends with Bilbo, all Baggins and no Took once more, in his own recovered home, handing Gandalf the tobacco jar. But Frodo returns a changed person, and the plot does not close: it stops, with Frodo leaving for the West and Sam, Merry, and Pippin with an untold story – hinted at, as if it were factual knowledge, in the appendices – before them, and a told story unforgotten behind them.

Even so, the relationship between *LR* and *The Hobbit* is close. The longer narrative repeats and reworks the pattern and elements of the earlier story. This may be summarized as in Table 1:

Table 1. Relationship of story-elements in *The Hobbit* and *LR*.

The Hobbit	*The Lord of the Rings*
Departure from Bag End	Departure from Bag End
The Trolls capturing the dwarves: rescue by the voice of Gandalf	The Barrow Wight: Rescue by the voice of Tom Bombadil. ('family history' in encountering petrified Trolls)
Rivendell	Rivendell
Crossing of Misty Mountains; choice of route underground	Failure to cross Redhorn Pass; choice of route underground
Dark journey underground	Journey through Moria
Gandalf fights and kills the Great Goblin	Gandalf fights the Balrog
Magic door of the Mountain	The doors of Narvi in Moria
Bilbo's escape into the light	Leaving Moria
The Eagles rescuing the party	Gwaihir rescuing Gandalf
Beorn and his horses	Rohan
Mirkwood	Fangorn
Spiders	Shelob
The Mountain: the stealthy hobbit and Smaug's watching eye	The Mountain: the stealthy hobbits and Sauron's watching eye
The Battle before the Gate; the arrival of the Eagles	The Battle before the Gate: the arrival of the Eagles
Return to a disrupted Bag End	Return to a disrupted Bag End

There is a noticeable similarity of motifs and structure between the two works. In every case *LR* develops, contextualizes in time and space, and motivates. We do not know or really care who Beorn is, or why he is as he is: what happens to Bilbo and the dwarves carries us forward. But the Rohirrim have a history, a culture, an identity. Shelob has a relationship to Sauron, a believable evil vigour, which the ghost-train spiders of Mirkwood do not touch. Strikingly, both books follow the same pattern of 'There and Back Again', the basic motif of the quest narrative in Romance. But whereas in, for example, medieval Arthurian romance the return is to a court that has not significantly changed while the hero has been absent, here the Shire has changed – less balefully in *The Hobbit* than in *LR*, but changed none the less. Moreover, the journey has changed the returner: Bilbo is never the same again, and has lost his reputation for ever. This is comic; but Frodo's heroism has led him to the point where he can no longer live again among the things he has loved, and this is near-tragic. Finally, the events on both journeys follow similar sequences. The central difference between the two books, however, is the Ring: in *The Hobbit* it is simply a 'magic' ring of invisibility, and its dangers are unknown. In *LR* it becomes the central symbol for the book's discussion of the attraction and the corruption of power. And the heart of that discussion lies, ultimately, in the Satanic figure of Melkor/Morgoth, once 'brightest of the angels', and in the tragedy of Fëanor and his sons in *The Silmarillion*.

A writer of 'fantasy' in the middle years of this century had no obvious rhetoric to use in narration as his predecessors might have had. A high style, in a modern context where we have no heroes, can too easily sound portentous, pastiche, or pompous; a middle style risks making the solemn and awe-ful sound everyday. The problem is serious, for what a reader first encounters in a text is not plot – that is as yet unknown – but texture, the surface of the narrative, the style. This syntagmatic level – how a writer chooses to express a meaning – conditions the reception of what is expressed. As Martha Nussbaum has pointed out (*Love's Knowledge*, 3), 'style itself makes its own claims, expresses its own sense of what matters. Literary form is not separable from philosophical content, but is, itself, a part of content – an integral part, then, of the search for the statement of truth.' Moreover, ideology, consciously or not, implicitly affects the choice of vocabulary: the values embedded in the words will come to condition the developing narrative.

Tolkien seems never fully to solve the problem of rhetorical level. Certain types of narrative, for one of his reading, would suggest certain styles, a rhetorical *decorum*. For example, the sacred poetry and the history of ancient Israel recorded in the Old Testament were written in a style the chief feature of which transferred comfortably into that used by the translators of the Authorized Version: parataxis, parallelism, or balanced, echoing syntactic units. When *The Silmarillion* deals with the genesis of Middle-earth, we hear those same patterns, often closing the syntactical unit with cadences that have roots in Latin rhetoric:

> But even as he cried aloud the light was blown out in the wind; wolves howled, and on his shoulders he felt suddenly the heavy hands of Sauron's hunters. Thus Gorlim was ensnared; and taking him to their camp they tormented him, seeking to learn the hidings of Barahir and all his ways. But nothing would Gorlim tell. Then they promised him that he should be released and restored to Eilinel, if he would yield: and being at last worn with pain, and yearning for his wife, he faltered. Then straightway they brought him into the dreadful presence of Sauron; and Sauron said: I hear now that thou wouldst barter with me. What is thy price? (ch. 19)

The archaism signals a high seriousness, and the occasional inversion, the elevated diction, suggest that we are reading the Scripture of Middle-earth: the style claims the importance of the narrative and our attention.

> Now I see that thy heart rejoiceth, as indeed it may; for thou hast received not only forgiveness but bounty. Yet because thou hiddest this thought from me until its achievement, thy children will have little love for the things of my love. (ch. 2)

This could be the Old Testament book of Genesis – but it is the genesis of the dwarves. The whole long book is consistent in this style which (because of its associations for the English mind) claims antiquity, the authority of the holy as well as of the secular power-structure of the Church, and the neutrality of true tradition. A narratorial voice is almost wholly absent from *The Silmarillion*: the whole is presented by an impersonal 'it is written', 'it is said', 'it is told'. But this stylistic strategy was chosen only after testing others: Tolkien tried many ways, ranging from heroic couplets to Menippean mixtures of prose and verse (as in the medieval *Aucassin et Nicolette*), and tested them on his friends. The final choice recalls not only the Old Testament but also the Old Icelandic *fornaldar sögur*, like the *Volsungasaga*, which, based on ancient myth, reach back to an oral tradition; and it suggests an uneasiness about the sorts of rhetoric, and their effect on reception, that were currently available.

While the style of *The Silmarillion* as published, noticeably homogeneous on a 'high' level, escapes the uncertainty of voice noticeable in *LR* and *The Hobbit*, this may be because in the first instance the audience was simply Tolkien himself and, eventually, a few sympathetic friends. But writing for publication, as in *LR*, is a different matter: no reading aloud to friends here, where tone of voice and physical presence do much; but an anonymous, undefinable audience, receiving through the eye. The unevenness of tone, the occasional slovenliness of metaphor or simile – faults which are absent from his elegant critical writing – may be due in part to this uncertainty about audience response.

Tolkien admitted that his children disliked the tone and style of those parts of *The Hobbit* which were written as if talking (down?) to children (see, for example, the letter to Walter Allen, April 1959, *Letters*, p. 297). The 'Ho, Ho' manner might work in the dynamics of child/adult conversation, where it offers a reassuring authority, but is awkward in cold print: 'Gandalf! if you had heard only a quarter of what I have heard about him, and I have heard only very little of all there is to hear, you would be prepared for any sort of remarkable tale' (ch. 1). The self-reference does not hide the awkward written relationship of narrator to reader. (In the first part of the book such direct address to the reader is common.) Occasionally the writing is slack, unvisualized: in chapter 1 Tolkien introduces Gandalf with 'long bushy eyebrows that stuck out further than the brim of his shady hat' – this is a grotesque, if pictured. Event is sometimes not handled much better:

> The yells and the yammering, croaking, jibbering and jabbering; howls, groans and curses, shrieking and skriking, that followed were beyond description. Several hundred wild cats and wolves being

roasted slowly alive together would not have compared with it. (ch. 4)

What is the point of (and how credible is) the simile of the roasted cats and wolves? The alliterative pairing of verbs is clumsy and contrived. But later the narratorial presence becomes less obtrusive, and more weight is thrown onto the dialogue and the action – 'showing' rather than 'telling' – and the tone shifts: the homely jolliness of the early chapters disappears, and we get something much more suggestive of great events with great consequences. One can see Tolkien almost 'learning on the job'.

The Lord of the Rings presents the greatest stylistic problems, precisely because it designedly draws together, as part of its serious moral purpose, different worlds of words: a countryside visualized like a pre-war England of stable social structure, where cheerful rustics gossip over their beer, and the councils among the great in an aristocratic warrior society; landscapes of horror, like the Dead Marshes; the terrible beauty of Lothlórien; the slag-heap ugliness of the Black Land – Black Country? – of Mordor. One of the most interesting things that Tolkien has done is to take the faerie world of medieval romance and earth it to the everyday – as Spenser, or Ariosto, or Malory never did or had to. But to get stylistically from the everyday to the high heroic, in an age when the high heroic mode no longer exists as a convention, and to retain, at the same time, the reader's confidence, is not easy. Much depends on the relationship Tolkien can create with his audience as he moves between the naturalistic narrative, with a good deal of dialogue, among the rustic hobbits of the first chapter to the solemnity of chapters like 'The Field of Cormallen' or 'The Steward and the King'. In between he has to create a decorous sort of utterance for his creatures: something treeish for Fangorn (whose booming voice was based, apparently, on Lewis's); a heroic verse for the Rohirrim; speech of dignity and weight for the great ones of the Noldor, like Galadriel; speech that reflects the depravity of the Orcs. Indeed, Tolkien seems to link speech and utterance to the moral nature of characters and their potential for moral choice. For of the nine talking species in his world, the unfallen Elves, the Dwarves, Hobbits, Men, Wizards, Ents – all capable of good or evil – have languages both complex and capable of parabolic utterance in poetry. The Trolls and Orcs, by contrast, are capable

44

only of evil, and cannot imagine good motives: what we hear of their utterance suggest their languages themselves are ungrammatical, irrational, debased in vocabulary and elocution. And in Gollum the common speech he shares with Bilbo and Frodo has, over time and in his self-absorbed, torturing desire under the mountains, degenerated into sounds that are barely above mere animal noise.

But this is to anticipate. The style of the foreword with which the first edition of *LR* opened shows Tolkien's nervousness about relations with an unknown audience. It begins by repositioning the reader's expectations of what is to follow: the first sentence demands we accept what we know to be fiction as fact: 'This tale, which has grown to be almost a history of the great War of the Ring, is drawn for the most part from the memoirs of the renowned Hobbits, Bilbo and Frodo, as they are preserved in the Red Book of Westmarch'. The 'editorial' voice at the same time partly defers responsibility and also authorizes the ensuing narrative by locating its origin in a text, the Red Book, whose existence is, apparently, beyond question; and the hobbits (hobbits?) are 'renowned'. Similarly in the Prologue, 'Concerning Hobbits, and Other Matters': the fiction of fact is maintained by the pose (and the prose) of an editor presenting his text with the self-effacing efficiency of the introduction to *Sir Gawain and the Green Knight*. At the end, the appendices extend this fiction of the edited text, and cleverly supply, as sops to the curious imagination, many details of the background which the narrative could not include.

In the narrative proper, the strategic choice had to be made of the point of view to be adopted. A third-person narrative, with an omniscient and unobtrusive narrator, is the only way to control the whole mass of material – particularly, for example, the parallel narratives of Books ii and iv. Sometimes the narrator presents important events through dialogue, effacing his presence to allow immediacy of response at a critical moment. Tolkien also includes some substantial embedded first-person narratives. Those of Gandalf at the Council of Elrond (II, ch. 2) or in III, ch. 5 are important ways of supplying flashback information about Gandalf's heroic role and how he sees its function in the war against Sauron. In the first, too, Gandalf reads from a scroll, which records Isildur's own account of his taking of the ring from

Sauron's hand. Here the style has to be archaic, dignified, to fit the utterance of a king of long before: 'What evil it saith I do not know; but I trace here a copy of it, lest it fade beyond recall'. In that first person passage we glimpse the self-deception that led Isildur to think that he could safely keep the Ring.

On the other hand, sometimes the concentration on action demands a style almost without colouring or contextualisation. Elsewhere, Tolkien wants a different effect: grand, elegiac, sonorous, serious. This can be a simple matter of inversion or word-order, or the balancing of elements in a sentence:

> And afterwards when all was over men returned and made a fire there and burned the carcase of the beast; but for Snowmane they dug a grave and set up a stone upon which was carved in the tongues of Gondor and the Mark:
> *faithful servant yet master's bane,*
> *Lightfoot's foal, swift Snowmane.*
> Green and long grew the grass on Snowmane's Howe, but ever black and bare was the ground where the beast was burned. (v, ch. 6)

The measured balance of that last sentence, its patterned alliteration, recall deliberately the structures of Anglo-Saxon verse as Snowmane's people recalled their culture. Similarly, Tolkien put the Rohirrim's heroic poetry into the alliterative verse of epic Anglo-Saxon poetry, with a preponderance of co-ordinate statements with verbs in the indicative mood. A poem like *Beowulf* uses a paratactic style, full of appositional phrases, allusive metonyms; it also uses structural elements, conventional *topoi*, where the audience already have expectations. We can see traces of this in *LR*: for example, when Gandalf confronts Grima at Meduseld (III, ch. 6) in a formal, public *flyting* (quarrel) before Théoden and his court, one recalls the flyting of Unferth and Beowulf at Heorot.

When Tolkien read Book VI, chapter 4, 'The Field of Cormallen', to Lewis, apparently neither could hold back their tears. This is designedly the great moment of eucatastrophe in the whole work. Tolkien's stylistic strategy here resembles that of William Morris faced with similar problems in his translations from Old Norse: a style that echoes the measured parataxis of Malory, with an accompanying lift of linguistic register and deliberate archaism (in this quotation, 'land' is used in the sense of 'laund' in Middle English – an open space.)

46

So they came to a wide green land, and beyond it was a broad river in a silver haze, out of which rose a long wooded isle, and many ships lay by its shores. But on the field where they now stood a great host was drawn up, in ranks and companies glittering in the sun. And as the Hobbits approached swords were unsheathed, and spears were shaken, and horns and trumpets sang, and men cried with many voices and in many tongues....

On the throne sat a mail-clad man, a great sword was laid across his knees, but he wore no helm. As they drew near he rose. And then they knew him, changed as he was, so high and glad of face, kingly, lord of Men, dark-haired with eyes of grey.

The juxtaposition of this with the next paragraph many find greatly moving: 'Frodo *ran* to meet him, and Sam followed close behind. "Well, if this *isn't* the crown of all!" he said. "Strider, or *I'm* still asleep!"' (my italics). The static dignity sets off the impulsive, affectionate action; the high style and the familiar, with contractions and nicknames, reinforce each other. (It also reinforces the central theme, which we shall examine, of the importance of the little people, the unimportant.)

Yet even in this highly charged moment, Tolkien reminds us of the ambiguous nature of the narrative: of all narrative, of how story is within story within story, until we reach The Story. The omniscient narrator is, the foreword implies, relying on a text which is a *report* of 'reality'; Denethor, Treebeard, and Théoden are aware of 'stories' from the past as a means of knowing the present. Frodo and Sam, on the slopes of Mount Doom, wonder if anyone will make stories about them:

What a tale we have been in, Mr Frodo, haven't we?...I wish I could hear it told! Do you think they'll say: *now comes the story of Nine-fingered Frodo and the Ring of Doom?* And then everyone will hush, like we did, when in Rivendell they told us the tale of Beren One-Hand and the Great Jewel.

The future indicative 'will hush', which turns the wondering into a certainty, is fulfilled a few pages later, as the

minstrel of Gondor stood forth, and knelt, and begged leave to sing. And behold! he said:

'Lo! lords and knights and men of valour unashamed, kings and princes, and fair people of Gondor, and Riders of Rohan, and ye sons of Elrond, and Dúnedain of the North, and Elf, and Dwarf, and greathearts of the Shire, and all free folk of the West, now listen to my lay. For I will sing to you of Frodo of the Nine Fingers and the Ring of Doom'.

Before the 'true' story is over it is turning into legend, the matter of epic poetry, introduced with the conventional formula of the *scop* or bard calling for attention. And by Sam's mention of the lay of Beren and Lúthien heard at Rivendell, Tolkien neatly draws to its conclusion the process of the quest first set up in the council of Elrond, Beren and Lúthien's descendant, and links the Ring-quest and the defeat of Sauron with the humbling of Morgoth and the wresting of the Silmaril from his Crown. Future and past struggles against tireless evil that threatens the free peoples are linked in song.

The stylistic strategies of *LR* are resourceful. They are not uniformly successful. Occasionally they are unwittingly comic. (How *could* one respond to a greeting like Goldberry's 'Laugh and be merry'? What have the worried hobbits to laugh *about*?) Just as in *The Hobbit*, there are clichéd, clumsy passages, betraying a lack of sharp vision of the material: 'A heavy silence fell in the room. Frodo could hear his heart beating' (I, ch. 2). Descriptions of the natural setting are sometimes overwrought, even lush, in the poetry; but in *LR* they can be rather tired. For example: 'Away eastward the sun was rising red out of the mists that lay thick on the world. Touched with gold and red the autumn trees seemed to be sailing rootless in a shadowy sea' (I, ch. 3); 'his bed was of fern and grass, deep and soft and strangely fragrant. The sun was shining through the fluttering leaves, which were still green upon the tree' (I, ch. 4). Can the simile in the first example be made to work? Both passages gesture towards a very general-ized idea of waking up on a fine morning: but the *words* do not make us *feel* that morning. Similarly, in chapter 2, when Frodo and Gandalf are at breakfast, outside, 'Everything looked fresh, and the new green of Spring was shimmering in the fields and on the tips of the trees' fingers'. *How* it looked fresh is left to us; 'Spring shimmering' is pretty stale; 'the tips of the trees' fingers' sounds (despite the anticipation of the Ents) merely precious. In the inn at Bree, the room is small and cosy, the fire bright, the chairs comfortable – the hobbits may be presumed to feel relief, reassurance, comfort in the room after their journey, but there is little of the experience of those feelings. Yet this 'thin' description is adequate for its purpose, which is to sketch a frame round the real business. For example, when Frodo and Gandalf talk in Book I, chapter 2, there is hardly any attempt to describe the physical setting. What they are talking *about* is what matters to Tolkien, and *in the narrative* that is what matters to the readers.

It is noticeable how Tolkien relies in *LR* (more than in *The Hobbit*) on the maps to articulate a setting for the narrative, and on references to other episodes in his mythological cycle to colour that setting. Yet in the later chapters there is some attempt to represent something of Frodo's and Sam's consciousness in Mordor. In Book IV, ch. 10, a passage of soliloquy – almost the rhetorical device of *ratiocinatio* – shows Sam wrestling with his responsibilities. For Frodo, the landscape of Mordor becomes an analogue of his inner desert, as the barriers between his mind and Sauron's power weaken further. Tolkien uses more frequently an empathetic narrative style representing the character's perception – the 'was/now' paradox comes into play for vividness: 'Frodo was alive and taken by the enemy' – Sam's realization, not the reader's.

> There was a path, but how he was to get up the slope to it he did not know. First he must ease his aching back.... Now the miserable creature was right under her...there [Shelob] crouched, her shuddering belly splayed upon the ground...as she gathered herself for another spring – this time to crush and sting to death: no little bite of poison to still the struggling of her meat...the dreadful infection of light spread from eye to eye.

This section, the last quest to the Dark Tower, differs considerably in this respect from the earlier ones because its key theme is the triumph of the will over circumstance.

The Lord of the Rings also, like *The Hobbit*, includes a number of poems. Some say Tolkien was more poetaster than poet. Some of the early verse is certainly embarrassing, to our taste, though pretty much of a piece with the tweeness of some of Rackham's illustrations and of some contemporary verse:

I am off down the road
Where the fairy lanterns glowed
And the little pretty flittermice are flying:
A slender band of grey
It runs creepily away
And the hedges and the grasses are a-sighing.

(There is yet more of this poem, 'Goblin-feet', which he wrote about 1914). About then too, he wrote 'The Man In The Moon Came Down Too Soon', which eventually appeared in *The Adventures of Tom Bombadil* (1962), and despite the clever patterning of sound and internal rhymes which children love, did not add much to his reputation. Indeed, to make great claims on any terms for a lot of the poems that appear in *The Hobbit* and *LR* is difficult. (Many find the verse treatments of the Beren and Lúthien story weaker than the prose.) Again, one suspects the same uncertainty about the balance between manner, matter, and mode we noticed in the fiction as a whole. Sometimes the diction is weak; and the rare imagery can be vapid, though the versification is sure-footed enough. For example, the first poem in *The Hobbit* is a sonnet, with four-stressed lines of irregular length. The mixture of anapaestic, amphibrachic, trochaic, and iambic feet sounds energetic, gives it a (Tolkien would say) Dwarvish feel. But what conventional sonnet is about washing up? Some of the Elvish poems have a sonic and rhythmic structure which is beautiful, and echo the verse forms of the Finnish *Kalevala*: Tolkien had a good ear. But few except the real aficionados know enough Sindarin or Quenya to know what they are about; or how faithful the translation has been.

It is a different matter with the alliterative verse, which Tolkien wrote all his mature life. A version in that form of the passing of Arthur was planned; the incomplete *Lay of the Children of Húrin* (in *Lays of Beleriand*) is 817 lines of assured writing that is far more than pastiche. His *The Homecoming of Beorhtnoth, Beorhthelm's Son*, the radio play written by about 1945, is a sort of sequel to the Anglo-Saxon poem *The Battle of Maldon*, and is (appropriately) in excellent alliterative verse, a modern version of the *Beowulf* metre. In *LR*, the poems associated with Rohan use alliterative verse, entirely decorous to the society of Rohan. One might object that it remains excellent pastiche, just as the society of the horse-taming

Rohirrim remains distant from mid-twentieth-century Western experience. Yet here the organic appropriateness of the one to the other, especially for those who have some awareness of what a 'heroic' society was like as recorded in its poetry, validates each. The same cannot be said of the Elves' songs in Rivendell in *The Hobbit*: too much like 'Goblin Feet', they address neither real issues nor a believable unreal world.

The poems only really work when tightly linked to their narrative contexts, to heighten that moment. Though even in context success is not universal – some of the poems weaken and distract – the best verse does ennoble the narrative: illuminates it, indeed. The poems pause the narrative, much as an illustration does; and one could in, say, *The Hobbit*, consider the effect of Tolkien's illustrations and his poems together. (It is worth recalling the fashion in the earlier years of this century to design illustrations as integral parts of a work of fiction, often focusing aspects of it.) Tolkien, in fact, did make substantial numbers of illustrations for his work, done in strong unshaded colours, as in medieval manuscripts and heraldry. Some (as in *The Hobbit*) illustrated incidents where the picture of, for example, Bilbo and the Trolls saves much verbal detailing; and Tolkien's interest in articulating his world naturally led to its mapping. Those maps are not mere decoration: they have a deliberate, if cartographically clumsy, likeness-yet-unlikeness to the configuration of Western Europe, a suggestion that this is and is not our world. We are told in several places that great cataclysms have changed the face of Middle-earth, not least the Atlantean drowning of Númenor. Those maps, endpapers or fold-out maps placing the narratives they enclose in the world untold in the book, suggest, as does the unfinished time-travel story, *The Lost Road*, that England and Middle-earth are in some way related in historical time and space.

But the maps, providing a context and spatial relationship unexplored in the text, still leave room for the reader to cooperate in the fiction. In 'On Fairy Stories' Tolkien argued that literature speaks from mind to mind – by contrast, drama proceeds from mind via the shown object/incident to mind. The reader confronted with the word 'bread' 'pictures bread in some form of his own', and reading is an essentially co-operative endeavour. Everyone has an idea of what is a hill, what is comfortable, and these ideas will differ in accidents. But they will relate to an idea of Comfort, of Hills, of Bread. Tolkien is not interested in stopping us to consider this peculiar chair, or this peculiar tree: he wants us to read on, co-operating in the fable, filling in our own white spaces in the maps. Fuller description would simply weaken its onward thrust. Narrative shape is paramount. (It is, indeed, worth asking how descriptive is the Bible, or *Beowulf*, or Malory; and whether we would wish them more so.) Tolkien was not setting out to write 'Literature', with all that suggests of modern assumptions – though he may, with growing certainty, have been setting out to write mythology. And what might be a weakness in the one might be beside the point in the other.

Creators people their worlds by an act of words. But in the vast length of *The Hobbit* and *LR*, only a few characters can be said to be anywhere near 'characterized' in a normal sense: Bilbo, Sam, Frodo, Gandalf, and perhaps Aragorn. The few women are almost ciphers. Yet in his own mind Tolkien clearly did visualize most of his characters pretty sharply; the emotional commitment given to the reworking of Beren, or Lúthien, over the years implies as much, and from (e.g.) letters 244, 246, 247 of 1963 (*Letters*, 323–35), it is clear that Tolkien had a well-rounded view of his characters, their psychology, even their upbringing: he speaks as if they were personally known to him. But his writing about them, visually vague, hardly gives a coherent description. Even with the major figures in *LR*, the reader is left to do a lot of the work.

Probably this is a good thing. It is precisely that vagueness that allows us to project our own ideas onto them. If we are not told exactly what a hobbit or a Dwarf or an Elf or a Troll was like, we make them up for ourselves. Lewis stressed how useful was such vagueness in story where the ultimate interest is moral: non-human figures are

> an admirable hieroglyphic which conveys psychology, types of character, more briefly than novelistic presentation and to readers whom novelistic presentation could not reach. ('On Three Ways of Writing for Children' p. 27) Much that in realistic work would be done by 'character delineation' is done in fantasy by making the character an elf, a dwarf...the imagined beings have their insides on the outside: they are visible souls. (review of *LR* in *Time and Tide*)

Lewis wrote that well after he knew what Tolkien was up to, and after he had himself begun his own series of fantasies where humans meet Talking Animals, and monsters, and giants. Such 'hieroglyphs' occupy much of the action of *LR*, and of *The Hobbit*. With Elves and Dwarves, even Trolls and Dragons, Tolkien can build on some pre-existing assumptions. With hobbits, and Ents, he has to start from scratch. He does each in quite different ways. With the Ents (III, ch. 4), there is an element of surprise, a physical description more detailed and systematic than usual, relying on narratorially-conveyed detail and then, immediately, by the quoting of Pippin's much later, subjective account of his (remembered) 'first impression' of Treebeard's eyes, 'brown, shot with a green light'. But the key element is the *speech* given to Treebeard, a speech as slow and complex – did Tolkien think of it as an agglutinative language, like Inuit? – as the growth of a tree itself: language expressing nature and a way of being. The Hobbits, by contrast, get an editorial introduction, in *LR*, outside the narrative (and building on *The Hobbit*). The stylistic level chosen is far from subjective: it is neutral, scholarly, objective – and by using the present tense asserts its objective 'truthfulness': 'Hobbits *are* an unobtrusive but very ancient people' (if we have not seen one, it is because we have not been looking hard enough). This is necessary not only because of the centrality of Frodo and his companions to the narrative, but also because of the way Tolkien has used their society, in the Shire, to earth the fantasy to the real world. For the Shire is, recognizably, a vision – partial, nostalgic, limited – of an England Tolkien saw as threatened if not already lost.

Yet there are few physical details: stature, hairy feet, colours, a few habits. (Nobody in Tolkien's fiction looks closely at anyone else's face or eyes.) More important is the *suggestion* of a temper of mind: we are told they have 'mouths apt to laughter', but they are not seen laughing much. The hobbits' society is that of middle-class middle England, seen from the comfort of a well-stocked table and a room with a view over the village: rural, with no hint (until Saruman gets to work) of industrialization, a reassuring class system, willing gardeners, deferential rustics, and a private income. They are archetypically the Little People 'who have not spoken yet', taking little interest in 'Adventure' and what goes on outside their borders, comfortable, complacent, and smug: vulnerably so. Unimportant, often ignored, underestimated, on them nevertheless great calls are sometimes made. In Tolkien's lifetime the little folk of England had risen to such calls in the World Wars, and changed history. But in *The Hobbit* the seriousness of *LR* was as yet unsuspected: there Bilbo starts as cheerful, amiable, increasingly resourceful, generous, honest – a good exemplar/hero for the children's audience. But he comes to show profounder qualities: a capacity for compassion with Gollum, a willingness to take risks for others, imaginatively resourceful (as with the spiders or in the Elven King's halls) and able to act decisively and selflessly, as when he gives away the Arkenstone. Even so, he remains an unheroic, often undignified, unglamorous hero – which is part of the point – and only just this side of the ludicrous: if detailed description allowed us to *picture* his furry-footed rotundity in a coat of mail and a helm, it would be difficult to take it seriously.

The first chapter of *LR* shows the same Bilbo; but when we next see him he is ageing, he whines, and there is a terrible moment when Frodo sees 'a little wrinkled creature with a hungry face and groping hands' (II, ch. 1). After this, we can understand how a Bilbo or a Frodo, under the influence of the Ring, could turn into a Gollum. Even so, Bilbo is still capable of heroic gesture: in the Council he surprises everybody by volunteering to take on the Quest of the Ring.

In Frodo Tolkien takes the matter further. Only here and in Sam, perhaps, does Tolkien gives us something approaching full characterization. His name in Anglo-Saxon means 'wise, prudent, skilful': as often (not always) for Tolkien, to name is to know – if you know the language of the name. From the start Frodo is the more dignified: one cannot imagine Bilbo speaking with the measured solemnity, unabbreviated by colloquialism, of 'I cannot read the fiery letters' when the identity of the Ring is revealed in I, ch. 2. On his journey he is treated more seriously than Bilbo was, both by his companions and by those they meet, like Gildor. Bilbo's compassion becomes in him something like genuine understanding as he tries to recall Gollum to his earlier identity as Sméagol; and just as Frodo had a momentary vision of Bilbo as little and broken, Sam (VI. ch. 3) sees 'these two rivals with other vision. . . . before [Gollum] it stood stern, untouchable now by pity, a figure robed in white, but at its breast it held a wheel of fire'. Returning home, Frodo does not draw sword in the Battle of Bywater, and he restrains Sam from killing Saruman. 'You have grown, Halfling. Yes, you have grown very much. You are wise, and cruel. You have robbed my revenge of sweetness, and now I must go hence in bitterness, in debt to your mercy.' As Aragorn grows in status, Frodo grows in moral stature, and in self-knowledge. He knows that the wound of knowledge 'will never really heal' (VI, ch. 9). Yet despite the interest of this development in Frodo, relationships with other hobbits are not done in any great detail: when in the last chapter Sam, Merry, and Pippin leave Frodo, there is more a gesture towards the abstract idea of Friendship than detailed grasp of what sundering a relationship might be like. Even with Sam the relationship is little more than sketch.

Sam has a crucial and heroic role to play, and it is interesting to recall that Tolkien in a letter to Christopher, in 1944, ten years *before* publication (*Letters*, p. 105), said he envisaged Sam as the 'real hero of the book... the most closely drawn character, the successor to Bilbo of the first book, the genuine hobbit. Frodo is not so interesting, because he has to be too high-minded, and has (as it were) a vocation.' He starts as a stock character and never, to my mind, wholly grows beyond it – the army batman and devoted manservant, knowing his place and happy in it; lovable, useful, selfless, utterly devoted to his master. In Frodo and Sam is an idealized picture of the officer/batman, gentleman/body-servant relationship as it sometimes existed in the lost world of Tolkien's youth and early manhood. But even here Tolkien plays with naming: just as Sam's father's Anglo-Saxon name Hamfast means 'stay at home', Sam's full name too has a meaning. But the only times we hear 'Samwise' in full in the text is when Sam, under the influence of the Ring, has a momentary vision of himself as a great lord. 'Samwise' means 'dull, foolish': this is the moment when 'Sam' nearly slips into utter folly.

What we see in Bilbo, Frodo, and Sam is development of a sort. It relates to a motif frequent in *LR* and suggested in *The Hobbit*: the revelation of a reality hiding behind the normal, and one which was pretty germane to Tolkien's philosophical outlook. At the Ford of Bruinen the hobbits see Glorfindel revealed in his power – no longer simply an elf on a horse. Aragorn is revealed as King; in *The Hobbit*, Bard is revealed as the heir of Girion; Gandalf is revealed as more than the grey old man the hobbits knew and whom their children thought a conjuror. There are more examples. But this does not mean that the other major figures go much beyond sketches adequate to the purpose of the *mythos*. Merry and Pippin are hardly characterized at all: we are told they become 'lordly folk', but do not see the changes inside that would imply. Aragorn is everything one would expect of a Faerie King – it is interesting to compare him with just such a figure in *Smith of Wootton Major*. Loyal, honest, faithful, he is taken for granted – 'Strider'– until revealed. There are no surprise developments in Aragorn. He is what he always was: Strider, the Ranger's cloak hiding the King. Gandalf, too, is what one would expect of a wizard, and there is a good deal of complexity in his role, and that of the Istari, in the whole story. But any rounding-out of his status, nature, and mission is done not in the stories but in the appendices, or in the ancillary material on the Istari published subsequently. There is also a change in how Gandalf is used after he returns from the dead. He seems to be less meaningful as a character, to be more a force than a personage. He 'has passed through the fire and the abyss, and they [the Black Riders] shall fear him. We will go where he leads' (III, ch. 5). The resonance of Aragorn's words elevates Gandalf into something august and dreadful: beyond personality, and, indeed, while we hear his story, we never see inside him as he tells it: it is a narrative.

Details could be multiplied. It is interesting, too, how in *The Hobbit, LR*, and *Farmer Giles* presents are used to define the gifts – the potential – of characters: an unusual, emblematic mode of characterization. Presents given at Bilbo's Party reflect on the recipient: Adelard Took's umbrellas, Lobelia Sackville-Baggins's spoons. Such presents relate to present and past. More seriously, presents are proleptic of some future quality. The old sword sent to Farmer Giles is a call to arms and to nobility: Caudimordax is not only used, but becomes emblematic of the power and justice of Giles as an independent ruler. Augustus Bonifacius gave away his Sword of Justice, his legitimacy, to a more worthy holder, who tackled real dragons, not Dragon's Tail Christmas cakes. Much more seriously, the unique *mithril* coat and helm given to Bilbo prefigures his heroic action and wise judgement in the Battle of the Five Armies, and his giving it to Frodo not only looks forward to his quest but also to its symbolism: a hidden, inner strength, like the breastplate of Righteousness of Ephesians 6, which, taken away from him in Cirith Ungol, leaves him open to the temptations of Despair. Círdan the Shipwright gave to Gandalf the Ring, Narya: 'with it you may rekindle hearts in a world that grows chill' (Appendix B). The presents of Galadriel explicitly express the nature and the future needs of those to whom she gives them: for Frodo, the phial of Light that shines in Darkness and is not comprehended by that darkness; the box of earth for Sam; the bow for Legolas from which flies the arrow that saves Aragorn at Helm's Deep; the jewelled belts for Merry and Pippin which, cast away, put Aragorn and Legolas and Gimli on their trail when the Orcs captured them. This throws an interesting light on the way Gollum/Sméagol calls his 'precious' his 'birthday present': the ring for which he killed Déagol draws out the flaws in him that in the end destroy him.

The patterning of characters seems to suggest some of Tolkien's thematic concerns. We noticed earlier a binary structure under-pinning the narrative, of journey/refuge, tower versus tower, The Shire set against Mordor, the Dead Marshes against Lothlórien – emblems not just of good and evil but also of corruption of the fair into the foul: and the *primacy* of the good. This extends to peoples and individuals. The orcs contrast with the Elves, the Trolls with the Dwarves – 'creations of the Dark Lord in mockery' of the Children of Ilúvatar, as *The Silmarillion* says. The narrative systematically focuses on paired characters. Each pair share common ground, including moral choices or challenges, and react in opposite ways. For example, each of the brothers Faramir and Boromir has the Ring-Bearer in his power, but their reactions are diametrically opposed. Saruman and Gandalf are foils to each other: each is capable of great good, and great evil. Aragorn is opposed to the Shadow of a Man who became Lord of the Nazgûl: the desire for, and right to, power could lead to either end. And Galadriel, most powerful of the Noldor still in Middle-earth, whose memory reached back to the theft of the Silmarils and beyond, is strong enough to renounce the chance of taking the Ring to defeat Sauron: 'You will give me the Ring freely! In place of the Dark Lord you will set up a Queen... I pass the test...I will diminish, and go into the West, and remain Galadriel!' Most interestingly, this pattern is seen in the hobbits. Bilbo's and Gollum's common ground is laid down in *The Hobbit*:

it is clear that they share a common culture in knowing the rules and material of the riddle game (as Gandalf points out in *LR* I, ch. 2). But in *LR* it is the relationship between Gollum and Frodo that most arrestingly acts as a climax to all the binary oppositions we have noticed. The idea of a *doppelgänger*, the double who is opposite yet integral, is a common motif in the nineteenth-century novel: for example, in Poe's *William Wilson* (1839), Stevenson's *Dr Jekyll and Mr Hyde* (1886), and Conrad's *The Secret Sharer* (1912). Gollum is in something very like this sort of relationship to Frodo: he is a shadow. Both bearers of the Ring, they are curiously attracted to each other: Frodo by pity and compassion, Gollum by the nearest he can now get to love. Their interdependence, the reciprocity of potential between them, comes to a climax in the Sammath Naur, when their bodies embrace in struggle. Both Sam and Frodo see something puzzling in Gollum: the potential to have been other makes him, as Sam puts it, two people, Slinker and Stinker. Gandalf and Frodo recognize that even in his misery and evil he deserves some compassion, and 'may have a part to play before the end'. As, indeed, he has, when Frodo fails in will at the last moment and Gollum's hideous desire for the Ring completes the quest – unwittingly. His evil had that purpose. His primal crime, the murder of his brother Déagol, his casting out like Cain, his wandering as an outcast, have led ineluctably to that end. A great irony surrounds his evil. As Augustine remarked, even the evil are caught in the web of good.

The motif of the divided self runs pretty deep in Tolkien's life and work. Bilbo was half Baggins, respectable, orderly, dull, and half Took, adventurous, unpredictable, surprising. He looked 'more like a grocer' but turned out to be a very good burglar. Gollum is also Sméagol the Hobbit. The pattern reaches back into the mythology Tolkien constructed, for Melkor/Morgoth was once not evil but good. Tolkien's own self was divided between the philologist and the mythologue, the analyst and the creator, and this shows in the uncertainty of the voices in much of his fiction. In his own life he was two people, and in his ancestry too. Took and Tolkien, Baggins and Suffield (a Suffield aunt, Jane, lived at a farm at Dormston, Worcestershire, called Bag End): between two worlds. Indeed, Tolkien must have known the medieval understanding of Man as a creature at the border between the world of sense and spirit, in the 'isthmus of a middle state', an *animal rationale*, who can converse with the angels (if he is lucky) and yet feels the needs of an animal. And in such a state, the inescapability of moral choice, and its profound importance, is stark.

4

Imperium and Cosmos

Tolkien's Christian understanding of the nature of the world was fundamental to his thinking and to his major fiction. Neither propaganda nor allegory, at its root lies the Christian model of a world loved into being by a Creator, whose creatures have the free will to turn away from the harmony of that love to seek their own will and desires, rather than seeking to give themselves in love to others. This world is one of cause and consequence, where everything matters, however seemingly insignificant: action plucks on other actions, and the end of this self-love is the reduction of freedom, the imprisonment in the self, and the inability to give or receive the love that is the only thing desired. There is common ground with other great religions here, like Islam or Hinduism; and, with them, Christianity sees the universe as a place of struggle between good and evil where individuals are crucial. And evil, though in the end it will be defeated, always has the initiative, just as in Renaissance drama the machiavel, who seems fair but is foul, always has the initial advantage over those who play by the rules.

In *The Silmarillion* and *LR* many of the strategic thematic ideas are Biblical. Melkor, renamed Morgoth by Fëanor, sets himself against the One or the Creation of the One, like Satan, once the brightest of the Angels. Melkor's corruption of the 'third theme' of creation, that of elves and men, mirrors Satan's of Adam and Eve; and his demand for worship, offered to him at his servant Sauron's bidding in apostate Númenor, is Satanic. The Fall is a key theme: a once-perfect world corrupted. And temptation: first Melkor, then Sauron, is the Tempter, and according to their potential, all other characters are tempted. Fëanor, most skilful of the Noldor, comes to value the works of his own hands more than the gifts that made them possible. The oath he and his sons swear provokes the Elves to crime upon crime against each other. Lust for jewels and gold draws the Dwarves in Moria to delve *too* deep because of their desire for *mithril,* and wake a Balrog out of the past (or subconscious) of the world. Among them, Thorin in *The Hobbit* falls into pride, avarice, and overwhelming desire for the Arkenstone, which warps his judgement and nearly leads to the Free Peoples destroying each other. Saruman, tempted by the desire for power over the world he was sent to help, becomes a poor copy of Sauron himself. He cannot fight Sauron with Sauron's weapons without becoming like him. Tolkien noted that in the real world the Ring 'would have been seized and used against Sauron . . . Barad-Dûr would not have been destroyed but occupied' (Preface to the 2nd edn. of *LR*, 7); Carpenter (p. 203) records his comment that the Allied bombing of Germany was 'attempting to conquer Sauron with the Ring'. Even Frodo in the end refuses to relinquish the Ring. But not all temptations succeed. Sam, though momentarily tempted by a delusive glimpse of what he thinks he might become with the Ring, spurns it out of love for and obedience to Frodo; Galadriel spurns it out of knowledge; over Tom Bombadil, in his joy of being, it has no power at all: the desire for power has never touched him.

Tolkien's stress on the individual is thus central. The *Beowulf* lecture was as much on the hero's moral and physical struggle, and its importance, as on the poem and its critics. His own published titles either name the Hero – the Hobbit, Niggle, Smith, Giles, Tom Bombadil, Beorhtnoth – or his adversary: The Lord of the Rings. It is the individual who is tempted by power according to his nature, whose choice affects eternity. But the heroes that succeed in Tolkien are not individualistic: they are all helped. When they decide to go it alone as individuals, as Turin does, it is a sort of tragic fault. Several – like Elrond, Galadriel, Denethor, and Aragorn – are as rulers open to the temptation of the short cut: to take the Ring, to go it alone, to impose by power what has to be constructed through love. Denethor falls. Noble motives and high courage lead him to attempt to combat Sauron's will directly, through the Palantir, and the end is a creeping despair that tells him the only hope for all his land stands for is military might, while his fury at Faramir's not taking the Ring is a measure of how it would have corrupted his basically noble nature: *corruptio optimi pessima*. But Aragorn, with every chance to take the Ring, refuses to touch it: the power it would give him would turn the true king into a tyrant.

Power and the nature of rightful kingship are major topics in medieval and Renaissance thought and literature. Arthur, or Charlemagne, encrusted as they were by legend and myth, were repeatedly used – as in *La Chanson de Roland* or in Malory's *Morte D'Arthur* – as ways of addressing the issue, which was frequently pressingly contemporary. One cannot read *Beowulf* with any attention and not see that the development of the hero into fitness for rule, and his discharge of that office, is a major issue. Beowulf's refusal of the crown when Hygd offers it is temperate, prudent, and wise. So is his later acceptance of it: he falls from that prudence later. The terms of the medieval and Renaissance discussion are set, in essence, by the Old Testament paradigms of David and Solomon (and neither is perfect), by the Classical one of Caesar Augustus, and by the New Testament one of the King as Suffering Servant Glorified, in Christ: the Christ of the Gospels and the Christ of Revelations. The major patristic discussion of the matter is in St Augustine, in *The City of God*. Augustine sets against the *rex iustus*, the wise king, the tyrant who is no shepherd of his people, who is ruled by the 'root of all vices', pride, or *amor sui* – 'love of self'. From Pride spring the remainder of the other Seven Deadly Sins: Anger, Lechery, Envy, Gluttony, Avarice, and Sloth. Now *The Silmarillion, The Hobbit*, and *The Lord of the Rings* are all pretty silent on matters of lechery and gluttony; but on the other sins they are eloquent. In *The Silmarillion*, Anger destroys Fëanor and his sons. Sloth manifests itself as despair: the despair with which Morgoth successfully tempts Turin and Húrin, or Sauron Denethor. Turgon's love for his hidden city of Gondolin is a love become possessive and selfish, unlike Aragorn's for Minas Tirith, which stands, a city on a hill, as a bastion against Mordor. The Dwarves become avaricious: their adversary and *alter ego* is Smaug, the embodiment of greed and avarice, who must be slain if they are not to be destroyed. Envy and despair of a happiness and love from which he has cut himself off drives Melkor, and Sauron (and Satan) to war on the weak, whom they set out to spoil to no purpose, and 'in the Darkness bind them' in everlasting sterility. The world – the real one, or that of Middle-earth – is a battleground of constant moral conflict far more terrible than anything merely material. The delight human beings can take in evil, and in inflicting meaningless suffering and destruction, amply evidenced by the Holocaust in our terrible century, is arguably more dreadful to contemplate than the actual suffering caused.

The figure of the Good King, Aragorn, knows the temptations of power, and masters himself and them. His reign is marked by a time when (as with Solomon) 'every man sat under his vine and under his fig tree' (I Kings 4: 25); the good beer and fruit of the Shire in 1420 are emblematic of good rule. His power recalls the empire of the Númenoreans before they listened to Sauron: 'the hands of a king are the hands of a healer', a teacher. His empire, like the *imperium* envisaged by St Augustine in *The City of God*, guarantees the freedom of individuals to seek the good while remaining the ultimate absolute authority. This political model is not fashionable today – though the existence of authoritarian states seems unaffected by fashion – but in many periods in history it has been seen as an ideal.

No fiction can satisfy every orthodoxy, least of all those that are differently historically conditioned from those of its own time. Tolkien's texts do reveal values that are Eurocentric, white, middle-class, patriarchal – those of the majority of his generation in England, in fact. They are values embedded in the very vocabulary of his work. The Black Speech of the Dark Tower – what we hear of it – echoes the consonantal patterns of Turkish; the Orcs' curved swords and their cruelty recall ancient legends, and illustrations, of the heathen East. The Southerners who come up the Greenway or fight in Mordor's host are ugly, slant-eyed and swart, emblematic of a culturally embedded racial stereotype of evil, the enemy; while the forces ranged against them, so far as we can see, are clean-limbed, white, dark-haired, grey-eyed examples of Northern European physical excellence. The societies the narratives endorse are either male-dominated, warrior-led monarchies – Rohan, Gondor – or a rural, yeoman, pre-industrial society of paternalistic power – the Shire, or Ham – where everyone knows their place and their speech patterns reflect it. (Trolls, when encountered in *The Hobbit*, have no manners, speak a form of Cockney, and have lower-class names.)

The overwhelming majority of characters are male. Love between male and female is not a major feature. Love for things, and places, and for family and friends is important: but Beren and Lúthien, Celebrían and Eärendil, Turin and Niniel, Aragorn and Arwen are about the only couples whose love gets much space. Even with Beren and Lúthien, the depiction of Lúthien's beauty is incomplete, indirect, the nature of their feelings is stated rather than explored. We are simply told of love: it is analysed neither physically nor psychologically. Tolkien is simply not interested in examining that area of experience, though one can be greatly moved by Lúthien's tragic choice. For what does matter is the shape and force of the story, the *mythos*, of which Beren and Lúthien – or Aragorn and Arwen, their descendents – are a part.

In *The Hobbit*, *The Silmarillion*, and *LR* male fellowship and supposedly 'male' values of heroism, courage, and endurance are central. Ancient heroic literature stresses male companionship, sworn brotherhood, and mutual support in danger and victory; but little is said of women. They appear, honoured indeed, tragic indeed, often able – like Hallgerd Hoskuldsdottir or Bergthora in *Njal's Saga*, or Thryth as we glimpse in *Beowulf* – to act and exercise great influence; but their destiny lies in the mead-hall or homestead. In the *Iliad*, Andromache's world and Hector's intersect, as such worlds did in life; but they are, in the end, incompatible, and the poem's weight is with Hector and Achilles. There was no place in the Quest of the Ring for major female characters.

Yet Tolkien does give glimpses of other possibilities. *The Silmarillion* tells of the heroic Haleth, first chief of the Haladin, leading her people on the terrible journey through Nan Dungortheb. The Stoors, Gollum's people, seem to have been matriarchal. In *The Silmarillion* it is Melian wife of Thingol whose power and wisdom guarded the realm of Doriath. In *LR* Galadriel is the only figure able to resist all enemies save Sauron himself. In Rohan we meet Éowyn moving through the mead-hall to offer the cup to Aragorn, like Wealhtheow in *Beowulf*, but we glimpse more than the passive endurance of the women in heroic literature. Éowyn's portrait is a moving cameo of a woman who knows she is trapped. For her, though a 'shieldmaiden', the *practice* of heroism, the ultimate values of her society, is impossible unless she discards her identity and becomes Dernhelm: and in that disguise, the unsuspected woman who is no man, she exercises a crucial influence in the Battle of the Pelennor fields, and by her hand falls the Nazgûl. Trapped by her sex and by her impossible love for Aragorn, her predicament is greatly moving.

But it can be argued that Tolkien is interested less in the specific social than in the generic human, and in the predicament in which mankind, not just men, or women, finds itself in a world of trouble and change. He transcends, in some sense, the ideological limitations of his milieu and reveals fundamental tensions. An important theme in all the major fiction is the inevitability of change and loss: an awareness that the best that can be won is an interim. (Another writer of heroic fantasy, John Heath-Stubbs, in his remarkable poem *Artorius*, 1972, suggests the same.) The moment of eucatastrophe at the Field of Cormallen precedes a journey to many partings, and home, where work is to be done. Lórien, in the end, will pass away; in the end, the Shire will be changed, and its cheery fairy-tale economy of mushroom-picking, tobacco-growing, and eating will disappear. *LR* is shot through with a sort of proleptic nostalgia for the things that will be lost. Indeed, *LR* links industrialization and the spoliation of the countryside with Mordor. Industrialization intrudes into the Shire when the old Mill at Bywater is replaced by a steam-driven plant, and when Sandyman, whose father was its master, becomes a mere employee of a cruel power-structure. The decorum of fantasy does not easily admit the direct confrontation of what such social change does to people – as Hardy confronted them in the terrible picture of Tess at the threshing-machine – but it can imply them, and suggest the mind-sets that are their fruit. Furthermore, *LR* and *The Silmarillion* do not shy away from the polarizing events of our century, the industrialization of war in 1914, the industralization of sadism and murder in the Holocaust, and the terrible potential of The Bomb.

In Tolkien's aesthetic, serious fiction, however fanciful, cannot avoid being in some sense 'true'. It must address questions of moral concern, significant to the diagnosis of the human condition. *The Lord of the Rings*, built on the inevitability of moral choice, recognizes the difficulties of such choice, and that all choice generates change, and cost. For Elrond 'even our victory can bring only sorrow and parting' (*Return of the King*, Appendix A, p. 342). The book offers a pessimistic, not despairing, examination of the human predicament in a fallen world at whose borders the dragons always prowl. Sauron represents something eternal; the war against evil is always unwon despite victories (II, ch. 4). Writing about the vision of the *Beowulf* poet, Tolkien described his own: 'The worth of defeated valour in this world is deeply felt. As the poet looks back into the past, surveying the history of kings and warriors in the old traditions, he sees that all glory (or as we might say "culture" or "Civilisation") ends in night' ('Monsters and Critics', pp. 264–5). At the end, Tolkien offers no facile happy ending. But nor is there simply pessimism: as has been remarked, 'Man's extremity is God's opportunity'. Tolkien does make the Valar respond to Eärendil's appeal; Gandalf does return; Théoden does once more find himself. An interim is won, and the stories (including this one?) of the kings and warriors, or of noble hobbits, fire the courage for the next struggle: 'despair of the event, combined with faith in the values of doomed resistance' ('Monsters and Critics', p. 265).

The ghosts of the Somme and Passchendaele haunt the Dead Marshes. The greed, malice, and sadism of Morgoth and his servants, the sheer will to evil, and its scale, acquire hideous significance after the revelations – those newsreels of Belsen and Dachau – of what men can do to men. Perhaps it is *only* in fantasy that we can now imaginatively grasp such horrors, avoiding desiccation into statistics or a slide into despair. And such evil, in the real world or in fantasy, has to be confronted: megalomaniac evil will not allow the choice to be non-combatant. The Hidden Realm of Gondolin cannot, in the end, stand aside. The Shire, protected, complacent, does not, in a sense, *deserve* peace, for it has not earned it. But it does deserve to exist. In the end it will be under threat; and comfortable, innocent Will Whitfoot will be maltreated by the storm troopers. The temptation to defend against evil by sheer power may in the end be too strong, as Denethor found out. Tolkien's vision of the struggle, in his fictional, old-fashioned world, allowed many to see (or think they saw) more clearly through its lens the issues they confronted in the world of the Cold War, in the increasingly materialist culture of the affluent West of a world where social norms were changing faster than they had for centuries. ' "How shall a man judge what to do in such times?" "As he has ever judged. Good and evil have not changed...nor are they one thing among Elves and Dwarves and another among Men" ' (III, ch. 2). No moral relativism here: rather, implicitly, a passionate restatement of the Christian view of man, of his nature capable both of glory and of utter evil.

The elegant *Farmer Giles of Ham* is a good place to finish this brief survey of Tolkien's major fiction. More playful in tone than most of his work, it echoes many themes and issues examined above. Like *LR*'s, its presentation is ambiguous, part of the fiction pretending not to be fiction. Tolkien in the persona of an editor prefaces the story with an introduction delicious in its pastiche of the rhetoric of scholarship. As in *LR*, the story proper is cast in a past and placed in ambiguous relationship to a real present where it is being read – Middle-earth to Europe, the Little Kingdom to Oxfordshire and Worcestershire. The Shire, glimpsed in *The Hobbit* and articulated in *LR*, is recognizable in the village and people of Ham, as the Misty Mountains may be glimpsed from Giles's and Augustus Bonifacius's expeditions to Wales. Just as the Shire is an idea of England transposed, this story too is located in a never-never England, in a remote period, which, though pre-medieval, has knighthood, and gunpowder for Giles's blunderbuss. Giles is an unpromising, unheroic hero like Bilbo – though not quite a gentleman. (He begins to acquire the authority of one later: 'the mare, for all her wisdom, had not yet understood the change in her master', 62). Like Bilbo, he discovers in himself unsuspected potential, and he too is lucky and shrewd. There is even the Gandalf figure of the wise Parson, who sees in Giles the potential for unlikely greatness. And there are serious themes in all this: the failure to discharge the duties of Lordship or Kingship in Augustus; the importance of little people; the necessity for courage and honesty. Tolkien stresses the intrusion of a parasitic central government on safe, comfortable, rural 'England', and the dangerous complacency in Ham as well as Hobbiton ('There's only one Dragon in Bywater, and that's Green') which ignores the real threat posed by Chrysophylax (who, after all, does eat people).

In the 1940s many felt alienated, thinking government

uncaring, stupid, wasteful. Hence the success during and after the Second World War of magazines like *Picture Post*, which voiced those ideas. Many resented the refusal of pre-war governments to take the threats of the 1930s seriously; many hated the centralizing bureaucracy of the wartime Coalition and the post-war Labour Government. Like Tolkien, George Orwell saw tendencies in politics, language, and society which he feared and loathed. His *1984*, published in the same year as *Farmer Giles*, offers a dark vision of the perversion of humanity, and its speech and values, by a monstrous tyranny. *Farmer Giles*, despite its lightness, points to the same sort of serious diagnosis that informs Tolkien's vision of the rule of Sauron.

Much of the humour anticipates a donnish audience. Tolkien assumes knowledge of the English Heptarchy, of the mythical history of Britain, of the styles of medieval salutations in documents. The cross-language jokes, too, such as 'Suovetaurilius' and 'Fabricius Cunctator', which are glossed as 'Suet' and 'Sunny Sam' (35), demand some knowledge of Roman sacrifice at festivals and Latin nicknames. Chrysophylax Dives (once again) is a name that expresses nature. Real place names get a fantasy history that is *philologically* plausible. The Foreword uses the tone and procedure of the critics lambasted in the *Beowulf* lecture, or of the fairy-story collector who tries to weigh moonlight of 'On Fairy Stories'. In his brief preface to M. B. Salu's translation of *Ancrene Riwle* (University of Exeter, repr. 1990, p. vi) Tolkien asserted that the translator collaborates rather than competes with the artist, 'endeavour[ing] to represent...natural, even cultivated speech...in modern terms', giving his work continuing life. Tolkien's parody editor, by contrast, here ignores the *story*, and feels he must defend his decision to translate this 'curious tale' on historical grounds: for the glimpse it gives of 'life in a dark period of the history of Britain, not to mention the light it throws on the origin of some difficult place-names'. Dismissively, he adds, 'Some may find the character and adventures of the hero attractive in themselves.' Then follows a patronizing discussion of sources and influences, and a censuring of the author for taking material 'not...from sober annals, but from popular lays'; [geography] is 'not his strong point'.

The editorial tone is beautifully done. Yet Tolkien builds in errors in the scholarship which quite subvert it. The supposed historian accepts the 'historians of the reign of Arthur' as 'sober annals', and the story that British history derived from Brutus as received truth. The introduction ends up constructing a tension between the *reading* and *use* of the text, and the 'story' – its onward drive and signification of more important matters. Just as Giles will not, in the end, be constrained by a supercilious Augustus Bonifacius *rex et basileus* – or by any remote government – the story refuses to be contained by this supercilious editor.

But this 'editor' is, of course, the artist. As in *LR*, Tolkien plays with deferral, simultaneously authorizing and de-authorizing his fiction. Some have seen this as a symptom in Tolkien of an irresolution between himself as critic and philologist and himself as artist. It may be no more than a game. But its effect on the reader is interesting, for it draws attention both to the story *qua* story and to the options that are open for its interpretation: reflexively, it suggests the provisionality of response, and the responsibility of the reader for it. Just as there is one sort of intertextuality, in Kristeva's sense, between *LR* and other texts in the Middle-earth corpus, so too there is a self-reference within a single text. The complexity of this, as it appears in *LR* and its wealth of commentary material, is elegantly anticipated in *Farmer Giles*, and playfully executed: but it is no less serious, for such editors do discuss the building of Heorot while the ignored dragons creep up outside. The pushing of *LR* back into a supposed past, from which the present is safe, allows the issues that are pressing to be fictionalized into historical note. But if they will not stay there...

Tolkien disturbs. He is fond of cutting the ground from under a reader's feet. How many have come to the end of *LR*, happy to return to the Shire with the Hobbits – 'just like us really' – only to be disorientated by the revelation that their names are not the comfortable English-sounding ones to which we attach sub-liminal associations, but quite other? Sam is really Banazîr, his father Ranugad, Meriadoc Kalimac. The familiarity disappears. The certainties of language – or what we take as certainties – evaporate: the philologist knows, and the storyteller shows, that though language is the only way we can make sense of our world, that sense – a life-and-death matter – is provisional. Change is the only certainty.

5

Responses

An author dies a little when he publishes. He has no further control over his work or how it is read, and it takes on a life independent of him. Readers and critics will construct what meaning in it they will, within what the text allows them: the author may even become hermeneut of his own work, not always consistently, as Tolkien's letters plentifully reveal. Moreover, what readers can make of the text will vary even within a few short years, as cultural epistemes change and mutate. Tolkien, on publication of *LR*, released something the nature of which no-one could have anticipated.

The Hobbit was in its seventh impression when *LR* appeared in 1954–5, but *LR* far outstripped its success. Reviews were mixed. From the outset it divided readers into those who passionately admired it and those who loathed it, and few were neutral. Auden, for example, admired it greatly; Edwin Muir, reviewing all three volumes in *The Observer*, accused it of irretrievable immaturity, heading his review, 'A Boy's World'.

But many loved *LR*. There were fourteen impressions of the first volume, eleven of the second, and ten of the third in the first twelve years, and it was not a cheap book. A New York publisher pirated it in 1965; which, ironically, only served to generate extra publicity and extra sales for the official US edition. By 1968, Allen and Unwin had produced it in various formats, including a one-volume edition on India paper in black limp covers in a slip-case: a format reminiscent of the Bible and major 'classics' of the canon. More than forty years later, none of Tolkien's fiction has yet been out of print. The demand for 'more of the same' meant that when *The Silmarillion* appeared in 1977, long after it was known to exist, an eager demand awaited it. Perhaps not since Dickens had a serious author achieved such widespread popular fame; and Dickens sought it, while Tolkien certainly did not. People stood on railway platforms awaiting the number of *The Old Curiosity Shop* that told of the death of Little Nell; people badgered bookshops and Allen and Unwin to find out when the 'new Tolkien' was due. Nearly twenty years after that, the material exhumed from Tolkien's papers and working notes is still appearing, accompanied by the sort of scholarly annotation that takes for granted the importance of its exegesis and of the development of the author's *œuvre*. Furthermore, there is a ready market for Tolkien calendars, song-books, notelets, paintings, encyclopaedias, and gazetteers. The quality is sometimes poor: yet publishers recognize that these 'peripherals' support the momentum of sales. And an interesting feature of Tolkien's success is how readily illustrators adopt the conventions of visual fantasy, from animated film, video, cartoon, and 'comic' to the illustration of a narrative which, as we have seen, is notably non-visual. The pictures of the Orcs, or of Treebeard, or of the Elves in *The Tolkien Encyclopaedia* are merely reductive: the resonance in the mind allowed by the text is damped down. But they still sell.

For interest in Tolkien has never flagged. Tolkien remarked to Auden (4 August 1965) on the foundation of the Tolkien Society of America, 'Real lunatics don't join them, I think. But still such things fill me with alarm and despondency' (*Letters*, p. 359). By the 1980s there were Tolkien Societies all over the world, including North Borneo, and a branch in Japan with its own logo. And such societies publish journals: *Mallorn, The New Tolkien Newsletter/The Road, Amon Hen* (the Tolkien Society of Great Britain), *Quettar, Anor*. There are periodicals dedicated to the elucidation, exegesis, and criticism of the texts, and exploration in detail of those languages that never were. Oxford's Bodleian Library in 1992 staged 'J. R. R. Tolkien: life and legend: an exhibition to commemorate the centenary of the birth of J. R. R. Tolkien (1892–1973)'. In the same year, Thornton's, the Oxford booksellers, published 'Tolkien and friends: the centenary 1892–1992: A catalogue of new and second-hand titles'; a Tolkien Centenary Conference was held at Keble College, Oxford, in August 1992, with learned papers, a thanksgiving service, and Oxonmoot 92 – fantasy world enjoyed by enthusiasts as well as more detached scholars. Relics are valuable: Tolkien's old gown was sold at auction in 1993 in London by Gekoski and Grogan of Pied Bull Yard for £850. And at the same time *LR* and *The Hobbit* have made it into the educational system: they are explicated in the various study guides, like York Notes, Cliff's Notes, and Monarch Notes. Much serious critical work has been devoted to the books. Not many authors so recent, without a radical new critical theory to their name, can have been the subject of international conferences: but in 1992, for example, at the University of Turku, Finland, a conference was held on 'The Tolkien Phenomenon'. Up to 1981, as West's bibliography records, there had been 27 Doctoral or Master's dissertations on Tolkien. Comparison with C. S. Lewis, who also has his Newsletter, Societies, and exegetes, only points up the differences; for Lewis's following is considerably influenced by his extra-literary reputation as a Christian apologist. (Lewis has already appeared in at least one stained-glass window.)

The initial popularity of *LR* was undoubtedly affected by a variety of non-literary and cultural phenomena. It almost exactly coincided with the peace gone sour, with (in Britain) the Aldermaston Marches against the Bomb. Many argued for the moral necessity of nuclear disarmament: casting the Ring into the fires. In America, in the 1960s, many questioned the use of power and the morality of foreign policy with regard to the running sore of Vietnam. For a few years a whole generation – especially the students – in England and in the US read off from Tolkien's books a political mythology for that time of a Cold War which could so easily have become a hot one. Graffiti – 'Tolkien is hobbit forming' – appeared on both sides of the Atlantic; 'Frodo lives!' graced the walls of a railway cutting outside King's Cross station in London; and in a lavatory cubicle in Cambridge University Library one was informed, 'This is Mordor'. (Interestingly, in *The Dark Tower*, 1977, an unfinished story in Lewis's Ransom sequence, Cambridge University Library is the model for the Dark Tower.) Months, even, after *LR* appeared there is evidence that its vision was not only becoming part of the conversational currency on which educated people could rely, but also offering a moral and aesthetic paradigm. In July 1956 a young Fellow of Magdalene College, Cambridge, Derick Mirfin, wrote to his mother about the new building that college's Council had decided to erect. He did not like it. He says that if asked his opinion by the Master, Sir Henry Willink, the distinguished civil servant, he will tell him 'that nothing so dreadful has been imagined by human mind since Tolkien gave us *The Lord of the Rings* with its horrifying description of Barad-Dûr – the Dark Tower of the Lord of Evil. The M[aster] is a great admirer of the book and the allusion will strike deep.'

Yet not all, by any means, admired or admire Tolkien's work. Rosemary Jackson (*Fantasy*, 155) suggested that Tolkien's 'high fantasy' functions as 'a conservative vehicle for social and instinctual repression'. Moorcock in *Wizardry* and others attacked *LR* as offering 'pernicious confirmation of the values of a morally bankrupt middle class... Winnie-the-Pooh posing as epic....Like Chesterton, and other markedly Christian writers who substituted faith for artistic rigour, he sees the petit bourgeoisie, the honest artisans and peasants, as a bulwark against Chaos.' Tolkien's prose was 'enjoyed not for its tensions but its lack of tensions. It coddles; it makes friends with you; it tells you comforting lies...The humour is often unconscious.' Nor did *The Silmarillion* ever win even the measure of critical applause of *LR*, getting on the whole lukewarm reviews. Eric Korn's witty demolition, 'Doing it by Elves', in *The Times Literary Supplement* for 23 September 1977 was followed a week later by Peter Conrad's in the *New Statesman*, who damned Tolkien in this new book as 'an unadventurous defender of mediocrity who can't write'.

One must take the criticisms seriously, for there is some justice in them. Yet others, equally eminent, found far more to admire than condemn. Critics with the experience and taste of A. E. Dyson could claim in a widely distributed audio cassette lecture (Norwich Tapes, 1985) that *LR* and Eliot's *Four Quartets* were the two greatest works produced in his lifetime, since the 1930s. What is interesting is not so much the evaluation (which can be questioned) as the field of comparison, which is becoming increasingly natural: for example, Pierre Jourde, *Géographies imaginaires*, discusses Tolkien as seriously as he does Borges or Michaux.

Lewis's review of *The Fellowship of the Ring* in *Time and Tide* in August 1954 suggests why some, at least, responded and still respond with enthusiasm:

In it heroic romance, gorgeous, eloquent, and unashamed, has suddenly returned at a period almost pathological in its anti-romanticism.... To us, who live in that odd period, the return – and the sheer relief of it – is doubtless the important thing.

Tolkien was, for some, meeting an emotional and intellectual need that modern fashion ignored. But, as we have seen, he had to invent a language to do it. The problem is that modern England and America have, from bitter political experience, abandoned the heroic. There is no longer a grand style in anything: certainly heroic public verse, of even the limited elevation possible in the early years of this century, cannot be attempted without risking scorn and sneer. Yet precisely this lack in society and in our scheme of values fuels the taste for Tolkien and his successors in the genre of 'heroic' fantasy: it answers a need in us all. It is that same need which, one fears, was met by the fake idealism in Nazism, a dream of terrible beauty and glory, a falsification and vulgarization of some of the ideals of Hegel and Heidegger. It is also an emotional need – for the simplicity of innocence, for moral clarity, for a cleansed world – that the more extreme claims of the Green movement speak to. And Tolkien, whose views about what is called progress and scientific and economic development were not kindly, was very soon adopted as a kind of prophet by those groups from whom the Green movement has grown.

This appeal was not limited to Anglophone cultures. By 1982, *LR* had been translated into Dutch, Swedish, Polish, Italian, Danish, German, French, Japanese, Finnish, Norwegian, Portuguese, Serbo-Croat, and Russian. The ingenuity, and courage, of translators attempting this text demands admiration, for it is not simply one linguistic problem, but several, and those are complicated by the differences in folkloric background between cultures. In the Slav cultures, for example, there is no word or concept for goblin: the Polish translator had to reinvent a world to translate the orcs, and had, moreover, no high style in Polish to use for important parts of the books. But the fact that such translations were commercially successful does rather bear out Tolkien's Jungian diagnosis of the faerye story as something archetypal.

Tolkien's influence has been profound on younger writers of

fantasy, many of them of the student generation for whom *LR* became the cult book. (Cult books get their tail pulled. In 1969 appeared *Bored of the Rings*, which put Frodo in impossible positions and predicaments with highly-sexed elf-maidens and others.) The market his works created welcomed others, who followed where he had led. The seriousness with which many took his work rehabilitated, so to speak, the genre of fantasy after a long eclipse. Some of the stuff that appeared and still appears – particularly in film, video game, and comic – is deplorable, of course: struggle and combat reduced to little more than voyeuristic sadism, where good is 'beautiful', over-muscled (if male) and scantily clad (if female), and evil revoltingly and not very plausibly ugly, in a world where, in the end, right is right because it wins: the moral thread has been lost. Sexual delicacy can be non-existent. But all high roads have gutters: at least Tolkien opened a road that some artists of undeniable quality have explored. Ursula le Guin's distin-guished work, the Earthsea sequence (*A Wizard of Earthsea, The Tombs of Atuan, The Farthest Shore*, 1968–73), has real complexity and profundity; in a quite different direction, the wit and intelligence of Terry Pratchett's stories operate in invented (cyber-)worlds where genuine human problems can be con-fronted. Tolkien's influence is also demonstrable on writers like Alan Garner, Susan Cooper (*The Dark is Rising* sequence, completed in 1977), Richard Ford (*The Quest for Faradawn*, 1982), and Robert Siegel (*Alpha Centauri*, 1980). Several of these writers (Cooper, for example) demonstrate, moreover, that good fantasy can be written from outside a Christian world-view like Tolkien's, and that it can be used to mount a critique of social, moral, and political assumptions. For fantasy destabilizes the cultural hegemony of the mechanistic model, necessarily political and associated with political structures, of the Western mind-set of the last two centuries. The resurgence of fantasy since the 1940s, much of it due to Tolkien's work, has coincided with decolonization and the emergence of pluralist cultures, and can be argued to have opened the road to modern modes of narrative like magical realism.

Furthermore, our culture is far more multi-media than anything conceivable in the 1940s and 1950s. Fantasy can be adapted to the medium of film, that dream, as Cocteau called it, dreamed by many people at once. Films like Steven Spielberg's *Close Encounters of the Third Kind* (1977) rely on changes in audience expectations in the generation for whose youth *LR* and *The Hobbit* were central texts. The common ground in all is the readiness not only to suspend disbelief, but the desire to accept, for the duration of the fiction, the reality of Natures not quite like our own. The extension of this into cyberspace is one of the most interesting developments of the last fifteen years: and the list of titles one can trawl from the Internet, and the way stories and games are presented, frequently reveal the Tolkien influence. The motifs of quest and heroic Last Battle are being more commonly used than at any time since the fifteenth century. Yet what sets Tolkien far apart from later fantasists is the stringency with which he approached the invented languages of his world, and the seriousness with which he articulated their background history.

The stridency of some of the adulation obscured, and still to some extent obscures, important things in Tolkien's fiction. Yet the surprising popular success of what is by no means an easy book, and is certainly not a perfect one revealed some important things about the culture that could respond in this way. The sense of a hidden significance in the book led readers to impose many allegorical readings on it which said as much about their own needs and values as about the book. Tolkien himself vigorously denied allegory (*LR*, 2nd edn., 7): 'I cordially dislike allegory in all its manifestations...I think that many confuse "applicability" with "allegory"... the one resides in the freedom of the reader, and the other in the purposed domination of the author.' Of course, we have met Tolkien the writer of prefaces being, in fact, a disingenuous persona, and that may be the case in this remark: this rejection of allegory could be an invitation to see if it will fit. On the other hand Tolkien, in the introduction to his translation of *Pearl* (published 1975, with *Sir Gawain and the Green Knight* and *Sir Orfeo*) sensibly remarked that to be 'allegory a poem must *as a whole*, and with fair consistency, describe in other terms some event or process; its entire narrative and all its significant details should cohere and work together to make the end...but an allegorical description of an event does not make that event itself allegorical' (18). The reader's response, however, is not wholly within the writer's control, so it is not surprising that many have tried to impose allegorical readings on Tolkien's work. But such readings have, in fact, rather proved his point: allegory – good allegory – demands that every single detail be taken up into the scheme of parallel meanings of a single notation, and this cannot be done with his work: the texts resist it. It is patently reductive, as Tolkien said many times, to see *LR* simply as an allegory of the Cold War and Mordor as signifying the Communist East, for example. He certainly disliked what he saw to the East, but Mordor is cosmic in significance rather than merely contemporary. The point is sharpened by noticing how identifications *reduce* resonance. For example: *lembas* could be seen as the Bread of the Mass, traditionally *esca viatorum*, for it has holy, even magical properties; it tests its recipient – Gollum does not like it; it heals Turin; it heals Frodo and Sam in Mordor. But there the resemblance stops. It is firmly a physical food, baked by the elves, not sacramental. Gandalf's time in the Pit of Moria – a name that in Latin means 'folly', delicately alluded to by Tolkien when he makes Celeborn talk of Gandalf falling into Folly (II, ch. 7) – after his battle with the Balrog is reminiscent of, but is not simply a rewriting of, Christ's days in the Sepulchre. Gandalf's struggle, exposure on the highest peak of Zirak-Zigil, and return, reminds just as much of Odin as it does of Jesus. The symbolic allows the reader and his recognition a part in the creation of significance, the allegorical denies that chance. C. S. Lewis's review in *Time and Tide* justly remarked, 'What shows that we are reading myth, not allegory, is that there are no pointers to specifically theological, or political, or psychological applications.'

But many tried. Some Christians (such as Clyde S. Kilby) have attempted to take over Tolkien as Christian apologist, as Lewis certainly was, and as Tolkien in his fiction certainly was not, reading off from the book straightforward doctrine. Tolkien's correspondence, and correspondents, indicate how powerfully the book generated resonances and significances, and how reductive he felt at least the expression of many to be. Replying to Father Robert Murray, SJ (2 December 1953), who had suggested that Galadriel resembled the Blessed Virgin Mary, Tolkien wrote: '*The Lord of the Rings* is of course a fundamentally religious and Catholic work; unconsciously so at first, but consciously so in the revision. That is why I have not put in, or have cut out, practically all references to anything like "religion", to cults and practices, in the imaginary world' (*Letters*, p. 172). In letters of April 1956 to Joana de Bortadano (*Letters*, p. 246–7), and to Herbert Schiro of November 1957 (*Letters*, p. 262), he commented that 'the real theme' of the book was 'Death and Immortality: the mystery of the love of the world in the hearts of a race "doomed" to leave and seemingly lose it; the anguish in the hearts of a race, "doomed" not to leave it, until its whole evil-aroused story is complete'; it was 'about Death and the desire for deathlessness'. These comments stress a sub-textual significance, and what at that point the author thought this significance was: it might be noted that the letter to Joana de Bortadano maintained that 'Of course my story is not an allegory of Atomic power, but of Power (exerted for Domination)', while Schiro was told 'there is no allegory...the tale is not really about Power and Dominion'. But each comment is inadequate to define the resonance of the book even for its author. Each response to correspondents who suggested a 'reading' of the book, with its differing emphases, reveals both how much it meant to him – he told Sir Stanley Unwin that it was 'written in my life-blood' (31 July 1947: *Letters*, p. 122) – and how aware he was that its importance and significance was limited by too explicit a reading. He saw it as a mythology for an England which, in contrast to Greek, Celtic, Finnish and Romance, and Germanic and Scandinavian, had lost what once had been. The very long letter to Milton Waldman of late 1951 (*Letters*, pp. 143–61) develops these ideas, and returns to some of the key ideas of 'On Fairy Stories' and the *Beowulf* lecture. But it goes further: 'But once upon a time...I had a mind to make a body of more or less connected legend, ranging from the large and cosmogonic, to the level of romantic fairy story...which I could dedicate simply to: to England; to my country' (p. 144). His creation of his world is in two senses re-creation: of a mind-set of postulated values and ideals lost in real time centuries ago, and also, in the case of the Shire, a personal ideal of an England lost at Sarehole Mill. The welcome given to it, and the many attempts of readers to articulate what it meant, suggests that Tolkien had hit some mysterious need. The taste for fantasy has to be Idealist, must search for Universals, whereas the fashionable temper of our times prefers the grainy, the gritty, the specific, the Nominal. We may as individuals train ourselves to be rationalist; as societies, I do not think we can. Destroy or abandon one mythology, or one religion, as has been done in the last few decades, and another, which might be very much worse, will take its place. Tolkien seems to have spoken to this spiritual need. This mythology of and for England seems fundamentally religious, keeping the rumour of the Other alive in a materialist culture and mind-set increasingly dominated by people like Nokes in *Smith of Wootton Major*. Many of Tolkien's readers wished to cooperate in his fiction of chronicles of a real world, and ended mapping their own by them.

Tolkien did the same. He came to live in his own fictions. When Edith died, on her tombstone was carved 'Lúthien'. When he too came to be buried with her, 'Beren' was added. The incompletable story returned to its beginning.

Select Bibliography

SELECT LIST OF WORKS BY TOLKIEN

This list does not include everything Tolkien published: such a list is available in West, in Carpenter's biography, and – a model of bibliographical exactitude – in Hammond (see below). Excluded from this list are research papers, minor verse and juvenilia, most journal articles.

Many of Tolkien's fictional works have been reprinted many times, and included in various collections. Citation in the list below refers to first publication; subsequent publication of the same material is not noted unless its context or content is significantly changed or the earliest publication is likely to be inaccessible.

Sir Gawain and the Green Knight, ed. with E. V. Gordon (Oxford, 1925).

'*Beowulf*: The Monsters and the Critics', *Proceedings of the British Academy*, 22 (1936), 245–95. Reprinted in *An Anthology of Beowulf Criticism*, ed. Lewis E. Nicholson (Notre Dame, 1963); *The Beowulf Poet*, ed. Donald K. Fry (New Jersey, 1968). Also included in *The Monsters and the Critics and Other Essays*, ed. Christopher Tolkien (London, 1984).

The Hobbit: or There and Back Again (London, 1936).

Farmer Giles of Ham (London, 1949).

The Homecoming of Beorhtnoth, Beorhthelm's Son, in *Essays and Studies by Members of the English Association* (new ser. vi, London, 1953). The poem existed by 1945. It was reprinted, with 'Leaf by Niggle', 'On Fairy Stories', *Farmer Giles*, and *The Adventures of Tom Bombadil* (see below) in one volume as *The Tolkien Reader* (New York, 1966); and again in one volume with *Tree and Leaf* and *Smith of Wootton Major* (see below) by Allen and Unwin in 1975.

The Fellowship of the Ring: being the First Part of The Lord of the Rings (London, 1954).

The Two Towers: being the Second Part of The Lord of the Rings (London, 1954).

The Return of the King: being the Third Part of The Lord of the Rings (London, 1955).

—— Second edition of all three volumes, with new Foreword, 1966. One-volume paperback edition, 1968. US editions (Boston, i, 1954, ii and iii 1955; 2nd edn. 1967; New York, 1965). Translations within ten years of Tolkien's death into: Dutch (1965), Swedish (1959), Polish (1960), Italian (1967), French (1967), Danish (1968), German (1969), Japanese (1972), Finnish (1973), Norwegian (1973), Portuguese (1974), Spanish (1978), Hebrew (1979), Hungarian (1981), Serbo-Croat (1981), Russian (1982).

The Adventures of Tom Bombadil and other Verses from The Red Book (London, 1962). This collection includes a good deal of his very early verse.

Ancrene Wisse: The English Text of the Ancrene Riwle, Early English Text Society, 249 (Oxford University Press, 1962).

Tree and Leaf (London, 1964).

—— 'On Fairy Stories', with 'Leaf by Niggle': a revised version of the 1936 Andrew Lang lecture and the story that first appeared in *The Dublin Review*, 432 (January 1945), 46–61. Reissued in London (1988), reprinted (1992), ed. by C. Tolkien, with the poem 'Mythopoeia'.

Smith of Wootton Major (London, 1967). Reprinted with *Farmer Giles* in one volume (New York, 1968).

The Road goes Ever On: A Song Cycle. Poems by Tolkien, set by Donald Swann (Boston, 1967; London, 1968).

Posthumous publications

Sir Gawain and the Green Knight, Pearl, Sir Orfeo, translated. Preface by Christopher Tolkien (London, 1975).

The Father Christmas Letters, ed. Baillie Tolkien (London, 1976).

The Silmarillion, ed. Christopher Tolkien (London, 1977; paperback, London, 1979). Translations within ten years of Tolkien's death: Danish, Dutch, French, Italian (1978); German, Finnish, Swedish (1979); Japanese (1982).

Pictures by J. R. R. Tolkien, with foreword and notes by Christopher Tolkien (London, 1979; 1992).

The Old English Exodus, text, translation and commentary, ed. Joan Turville-Petre (Oxford, 1981).

Unfinished Tales of Númenor and Middle-Earth, ed. Christopher Tolkien (London, 1980; paperback 1982). Translations: Dutch, Italian (1981); French, Swedish (1982), German (1983).

The Book of Lost Tales I, ed. Christopher Tolkien (London, 1983; Boston, 1984; paperback 1985).

The Book of Lost Tales II, ed. Christopher Tolkien, (London, 1984; paperback 1986).

The Shaping of Middle-Earth: The Quenta, the Ambarkanta, and the Annals, together with the earliest Silmarillion and the first map, ed. Christopher Tolkien (London, 1986).

The Lays of Beleriand, ed. Christopher Tolkien (London, 1985; paperback 1987).

The Lost Road and Other Writings: Language and Legend Before 'The Lord of the Rings', ed. Christopher Tolkien (London, 1987; paperback 1992). This grew out of a discussion between Tolkien and Lewis in the thirties about fantasy writing, where each agreed to try a particular genre. To Lewis fell space travel – *Out of the Silent Planet* was the first result. To Tolkien fell time-travel, and he seems to have been considering a format where the history of Middle-earth was a prehistory of the world as we know it.

Paintings and drawings

Scull, Christina and Wayne G. Hammond, *J. R. R. Tolkien: Artist and Illustrator* (London, 1995). Reproductions of Tolkien's water-colours and drawings, including artwork for jackets of *Hobbit* and *LR*. Range of his accomplishment is not fully represented by work in those books: the style of the illustrations there is clearly the result of deliberate choice.

Correspondence

Letters of J. R. R. Tolkien: A Selection, ed. Humphrey Carpenter with the assistance of Christopher Tolkien (London, 1981, 1990, 1995).

BIOGRAPHY

Humphrey Carpenter, *J. R. R. Tolkien: A Biography* (London, 1977, 1978, 1987, 1992). Still the most helpful and perceptive account of Tolkien's life.

—— *The Inklings: C. S. Lewis, J. R. R. Tolkien, Charles Williams and their Friends* (London, 1978; paperback 1981). The discussion of the friendships of, and relationships of thought and interest between, Lewis, Charles Williams, Barfield, Dyson, and Tolkien throws much light on Tolkien's development as a man and writer.

Tolkien, John and Priscilla Tolkien: *The Tolkien Family Album* (London, 1992). Portraits of the Tolkien family.

Diplomat (18 October 1966). There is a special section on Tolkien, including recipes for hobbit tables left empty by Tolkien: mostly of minimal interest. But see p. 39, the invaluable 'Tolkien on Tolkien', on his life and work.

BIBLIOGRAPHIES

West, Richard C. (ed.), *Tolkien Criticism: An Annotated Checklist* (rev. ed.), Kent, Oh., 1981). Absolutely indispensable. Records primary and secondary material. Full bibliographies and checklists. Cross-indexed.

Hammond, Wayne G. with the assistance of Douglas A. Anderson: *J. R. R. Tolkien: A Descriptive Bibliography* (Winchester, St. Paul's Bibliographies; New Castle, Del., 1993). Records variants within as well as between editions of all the works.

Johnson, Judith A., *J. R. R. Tolkien: Six Decades of Criticism* (Westport, Conn., 1986).

See also Rogers below.

FESTSCHRIFT

Davis, Norman and C. L. Wrenn (eds.), *English and Medieval Studies: Presented to J. R. R. Tolkien on the Occasion of his Seventieth Birthday* (London, 1962).

HANDBOOKS

Day, David, *A Tolkien Bestiary*, illustrated by Ian Miller *et al.* (London, 1979). Coffee-table. Drink the coffee.

—— *Tolkien: The Illustrated Encyclopaedia* (London, 1991; paperback 1993). Not altogether reliable; and the drawings vary vastly in quality. Some are deplorable.

—— *The Tolkien Companion* (London, 1993).

Duriez, Colin, *The Tolkien and Middle-Earth Handbook* (Tunbridge Wells, 1992). A listing of all the people, places and things of importance in Tolkien's writings; a mixture of factual reference and critical interpretation. As Sibley says in the Preface, you get your money's worth.

Foster, Robert, *Complete Guide to Middle-Earth* London, 1978, 1993). Complete, accurate. Rather solemn, if 'indispensable' (Brian Sibley).

Tyler, J. E. A., *The New Tolkien Companion*, illustrated by Kevin Reilly (2nd edn., London, 1979). Previously published as *The Tolkien*

Companion (1976). Covers a lot of the same ground as Foster.

LANGUAGES

Blackwelder, R. E., *A Tolkien Thesaurus* (New York, 1990).
Bradfield, J. C., *Dictionary of Quenya and Proto-Sindarin, with an Index* (2nd edn., Canterbury, 1983).
Allan, J., and Carson, Nina *et al.*, *An Introduction to Elvish: And to Other Tongues and Proper Names and Writing Systems of the Third Age of the Western Lands of Middle-Earth as Set Forth in the Published Writings of Professor John Ronald Reuel Tolkien* (Hayes, 1978). 'Authorized by the Mythopoeic Linguistic Fellowship, a discussion group of the Mythopoeic Society'. Includes an extensive vocabulary of Quenya and Sindarin.
Lobdell Jared (ed.), *A Tolkien Compass* (La Salle, Ill., 1975). Includes essays on various interpretative topics, and Tolkien's 'Guide to the names in *LR*', originally written for his translators.

CRITICISM

Auerbach, Erich, *Mimesis: The Representation of Reality in Western Literature* (Princeton, 1953).
Battarbee, K. J., (ed.), *Scholarship and Fantasy: Proceedings of 'The Tolkien Phenomenon', May 1992, Turku, Finland* (Anglicana Turkensia, No. 12, University of Turku, 1992). Indispensable. Good papers on the languages, sources, theology, and texture of his writing. See also Orchard, 'Tolkien, The Monsters, and the Critics', Shippey, 'Tolkien as postwar writer'; Tolley, 'Tolkien and the unfinished', examines Tolkien's debt to Rider Haggard.
Bettelheim, Bruno, *The Uses of Enchantment: The Meaning and Importance of Fairy Tales* (London, 1976; Harmondsworth, 1985). Psychoanalytic underpinning to argument. Importance of fairy tales as templates and models by which children cope with fears and problems, as liberating and supporting in maturing process. Chapter 'Fear of Fantasy' uses Tolkien's ideas in 'On Fairy Stories'.
Boccaccio, in C. G. Osgood, *Boccaccio on Poetry* (Princeton, NJ, 1930).
Briggs, K. M., *The Fairies in English Tradition and Literature* (London, 1967).
Brooke-Rose, Christine, *A Rhetoric of the Unreal: Studies in Narrative and Structure, Especially of the Fantastic* (Cambridge, 1981). Stresses the concept of ambiguity, openness, in 'pure fantastic' writing.
Crabbe, Katharyn F., *J. R. R. Tolkien* (New York, 1981). Detailed

examination of the thematic structure of *Hobbit*, *LR*, and *Silmarillion*.

Dante, *Convivio*, ed. Simonelli (Bologna, 1966).

Elgin, D. D., *The Comedy of the Fantastic: Ecological Perspectives on the Fantasy Novel* (Westwood, Conn., 1985). Ch. 2. on Tolkien. Argues the emergence of 'a new kind of novel'.

Fredericks, C., *The Future of Eternity: Mythologising Science Fiction and Fantasy* (Bloomington, Ind., 1982). Useful chapter, relevant to Tolkien, 'In Defense of Heroic Fantasy'.

Giddings, Robert and Elizabeth Holland, *J. R. R. Tolkien: The Shores of Middle-Earth* (London, 1981). Discusses *LR* in terms of its mythic as well as literary ancestry.

Giddings, Robert (ed.), *J. R. R. Tolkien: This Far Land* (London, 1983). Very enjoyable, useful collection. Walmsley, 'Tolkien and the 60s' is perceptive; Wynne-Jones helpful on structure of narrative; Robinson explores the lack of humour in *LR*; Partridge, 'No Sex Please, we're Hobbits: The Construction of Female Sexuality in *LR*' relates this important matter to Tolkien's friendships and views of the sexual relation. Final essay (Otty, 'The Structuralist's Guide to Middle-earth') targets the solemnness of Foster's *Complete Guide* (1978) and ends with a hilarious reading of Shelob's wounding by Sam as a sort of rape. (What one can do with language!)

Gray, Rosemary (ed.), *A tribute to J. R. R. Tolkien, 3 January 1892 – 2 September 1973* (UNISA Medieval Association, Pretoria: University of South Africa, 1992). Helpful essays on Tolkien's alliterative prose, the relationship of *Smith of Wootton Major* to folktale, voyage as symbol, and Tolkien's response to Wagner's *Ring*.

Helms, Randel: *Tolkien's World* (Boston, 1974). Discusses the theory of fantasy. Offers a Freudian reading of *The Hobbit*.

—— *Tolkien and the Silmarils* (London, 1981).

Hillegas, Mark Robert (ed.), *Shadows of Imagination: The Fantasies of C. S. Lewis, J. R. R. Tolkien and Charles Williams*, with an afterword on J. R. R. Tolkien's *The Silmarillion* by Peter Kreeft (1969, new edn., Carbondale, Ill., 1979). Four essays discuss T. Charles Moorman, '"Now entertain conjecture of a time"' compares Lewis and Tolkien, and suggests that Lewis's didacticism overwhelms his art, while Tolkien's Christian vision does not. Good essay by D. Hughes on 'Pieties and Giant Forms in *LR*'. Kreeft's 'The Wonder of *The Silmarillion*' makes great claims, and examines it (from a Christian viewpoint) in terms of Lewis's ideas in *Experiment in Criticism* (Cambridge, 1961) and *Sehnsucht*.

Hunt, Peter, *Criticism, Theory and Children's Literature* (Oxford, 1991). Interesting exploration of how critical theory and writing for children test each other. Passing references to Tolkien are provocative.

Hunter, Lynette, *Modern Allegory and Fantasy: Allegorical Stances of*

Contemporary Writing (Basingstoke, 1989). Powerful examination of genre and theory; helpful summaries of development of modern theories of fantasy and allegory; some shrewd remarks on Tolkien.

Irwin, W. R., *The Game of the Impossible: A Rhetoric of Fantasy* (Urbana, Ill., 1974). Covers the period 1880–1957. Analyses fantasy as an intellectual game.

Isaacs, Neil D., and Zimbardo, Rose A. (eds.), *Tolkien and the Critics: Essays on J. R. R. Tolkien's 'The Lord of the Rings'* (Notre Dame, Ind., 1968). The dedication 'For our Halflings' is not encouraging, but the collection includes important evaluations by W. H. Auden, C. S. Lewis, Robert J. Reilly, and Charles Moorman. Isaacs also addresses the choice of critical strategies. Auden's essay first appeared in *Texas Quarterly*, 4 (1962); Lewis's essay 'The Dethronement of Power' in *Time and Tide* (October, 1955); Moorman's in *The Precincts of Felicity* (Florida, 1966); Reilly's in *Thought*, 38 (1963).

—— (eds.), *Tolkien, New Critical Perspectives* (Lexington, Ky., 1981). Thirteen essays. Some relate *LR* to a variety of traditions; some examine Tolkien's own critical principles.

Jackson, Rosemary, *Fantasy: The Literature of Subversion* (London, 1981). Tough, theoretical, and Marxist. Fantasy as a distinct kind of narrative. Argues against transcendentalist fiction and criticism: such approaches are part of 'a nostalgic humanistic vision, attempting to recapture and revivify lost moral and social hierarchies': like any text 'a fantasy is produced within, and determined by, its social context...cannot be understood in isolation from it'.

Jourde, Pierre: *Géographies imaginaires de quelques inventeurs de mondes au XXe siècle: Gracq, Borges, Michaux, Tolkien* (Paris, 1991). Discusses the construction, mapping of and conceptualization of travel in imaginary worlds.

Jung, C. G., *Memories, Dreams and Reflections*, recorded and edited by Anneal Jaffé, trans. R. and C. Winston (London, 1981).

Kilby, Clyde Samuel, *Tolkien and 'The Silmarillion'* (Berkhamsted, 1977). Reverential. Writing as (and eager to claim Tolkien as) a Christian apologist. Speculates, perhaps unwarrantably, about what Tolkien *would have* written, and uses this as interpretative model.

Kocher, P. H., *Master of the Middle-Earth: The Achievement of J. R. R. Tolkien* (Boston, 1972; London, 1973). Shrewd and helpful discussion, good on characterization; discusses theory and practice of fantasy and Tolkien's interest in how spiritual and physical states relate.

Le Guin, Ursula, *The Language of the Night: Essays on Fantasy and Science Fiction* (New York, 1979; London, rev. edn., 1989). By a mistress of the genre, this includes her essay 'From Elfland to Poughkeepsie', discussing the relationship between fantasy and reality: she commends Tolkien's handling of this problem. Also 'The Staring

Eye': sees Tolkien as an outstanding fantasist, and underlines the challenge he gives to academic critics.

Lewis, C. S., *An Experiment in Criticism* (Cambridge, 1961).

—— *The Abolition of Man, or Reflections on Education with Special Reference to the Teaching of English in the Upper Forms of Schools* (University of Durham Riddell Memorial Lecture, London, 1946).

—— Review of *The Fellowship of the Ring* and *The Two Towers, Time and Tide* (August 1954); see also review of completed *LR* (22. 10. 1955).

—— 'On Stories' (1947: reprinted in *Of Other Worlds: Essays and Stories*, ed. W. Hooper, London 1966).

—— 'On Three Ways of Writing for Children' (1952), reprinted in *Of Other Worlds* (1966).

Little, Edmund, *The Fantasts: Studies in J. R. R. Tolkien, Lewis Carroll, Mervyn Peake, Nikolay Gogol and Kenneth Grahame* (Amersham, 1984). Theme of the book is the making and otherness of other worlds in fantasy, with reference to the authors indicated in the title. Chapter 2 on Tolkien.

Manlove, Colin, *Modern Fantasy: Five Studies* (Cambridge, 1975). Studies of Kingsley, MacDonald, Lewis, Peake, Tolkien. Explores split between scientific description of the world and the imaginative world of fantasy. Useful start for discussion.

—— *Christian Fantasy from 1200 to the Present* (London, 1992). Stress on genre. The brief discussion of Tolkien and the chapter on C. S. Lewis form part of a historical account of the development of specifically Christian fiction, and its present place in a world without unifying Christian vision. Learned, but some odd conclusions – claims that the victory of good is contrived in Tolkien, and evil is more interesting.

Montgomery, J. W. (ed.), *Myth, Allegory and Gospel: An Interpretation of J. R. R. Tolkien, C. S. Lewis, G. K. Chesterton and Charles Williams* (Minneapolis, Minn., 1974). Kilby's essay on Tolkien claims him as Christian apologist.

Moorcock, Michael, *Wizardry and Wild Romance* (London, 1987). Author is an experienced author within the genre. Chapter on Tolkien (first published as a pamphlet: British Fantasy Society, 1978), 'Epic Pooh', is one of the funniest of the attacks, and isn't without some justice, although occasionally degenerating into questionbegging and abuse.

Morus, I. R., M. J. L. Percival, and C. S. Rosenthal (eds.), *Tolkien and Romanticism: Proceedings of the Cambridge Tolkien Workshop, 1988* (Cambridge, 1988).

Muir, Edwin, 'A Boy's World', review of *The Lord of the Rings, The Observer* (27 November 1955).

Nitzsche, Jane Chance, *Tolkien's Art: 'A Mythology for England'* (London,

1979). Useful discussion of the relationship between Tolkien's minor works and criticism and the mythology developed in the major fiction.

O'Neill, Timothy R., *The Individuated Hobbit: Jung, Tolkien and the Archetypes of Middle-Earth* (Boston, 1979; London, 1980). Author, a military psychologist, read Tolkien under fire in Vietnam. Chatty, anecdotal, autobiographical tone wears a bit thin at times. Stresses value of Jungian approach, and rejects simplistic Freudian readings.

Nussbaum, Martha, *Love's Knowledge* (Oxford, 1990).

Petrarch, *Invective*, ed. P. G. Ricci (Rome, 1930).

Petzold, Dieter, *J. R. R. Tolkien: Fantasy literature als Wunscherfullung und Weltdeutung* (Heidelberg, 1980). Thorough discussion in ch. 3. of Tolkien's cosmos – 'applicability', Christian quests, theological, historical, and political aspects.

Plato, *Republic*, transl. and ed. F. Cornford (Oxford, 1941).

Propp, Vladimir, *Morphology of the Folk Tale*, trans. L. Scott, rev. and ed. L. A. Wagner; new intro. by A. Dundes, *Indiana University Research Center in Anthropology, Folklore and Linguistics Publications*, 10 (Austin, Tex., 1968).

Purtill, Richard L., *J. R. R. Tolkien, Myth, Morality and Religion* (San Francisco, London, 1984). Written from the viewpoint of a philosopher and logician 'for lovers of Tolkien'. Sympathetic account and reading of the works, with stress on ethics, myth and eucatastrophe. Some excellent close reading.

Ready, William, *Understanding Tolkien and 'The Lord of the Rings'* (New York, London, 1978). Originally published as *The Tolkien relation*, Chicago, 1968. One of the worst books to appear on Tolkien.

Reilly, R., *Romantic Religion: A Study of Barfield, Lewis, Williams, and Tolkien* (Athens, Ga., 1971). Very good discussion of Barfield.

Ridden, Geoffrey M., *J. R. R. Tolkien, 'The Lord of the Rings': notes* (York Notes, Harlow, 1984). A measure of Tolkien's now-canonical status: part of a series to help school pupils through (easy) exams. Chapter-by-chapter summaries, with glossaries.

Rogers, Deborah Webster and Rogers, Ivor A., *J. R. R. Tolkien* (Boston, 1980). Includes descriptive bibliography.

Rosebury, Brian, *Tolkien: A Critical Assessment* (Basingstoke, 1992). Two chapters on *LR*, one on 'Minor Works', overall assessment in 'Tolkien and the Twentieth Century'. Perceptive.

Rossi, Lee D., *The Politics of Fantasy: C. S. Lewis and J. R. R. Tolkien* (Epping, 1984). Discusses Tolkien's political despair and pessimism, and also Lewis's 'divided self', in the light of their common understanding of the Christian doctrine of original sin.

Salu, Mary and Farrell, Robert T. (eds.), *J. R. R. Tolkien, Scholar and Storyteller: Essays in Memoriam* (Ithaca, NY, 1979). *Festschrift* with essays on many of Tolkien's research areas, including a very important discussion by D. S. Brewer of *LR* as Romance.

Sammons, Martha G., *'A Better Country': The Writing of Religious Fantasy and Science Fiction* (Wesport, Conn., 1988). Written from a Christian perspective, reviews the historical development of the genre as well as examining recent work.

Schlobin, R. C. (ed.), *The Aesthetics of Fantasy Literature and Art* (Notre Dame, Ind., 1982). Tolkien discussed by Zahorski and Boyer, 'Secondary worlds of High Fantasy', and Crossley, 'Pure and Applied Fantasy, from Faerie to Utopia'. See also Manlove, 'On the Nature of Fantasy'.

Shippey, T. A., *The Road to Middle-Earth* (London, 1983). Arguably the best book on Tolkien's fiction. One of its major strengths is that Shippey is starting from the same academic perspective as Tolkien: he held the same Chair at Leeds as Tolkien once did. Shippey argues strongly for the timeless importance of *LR*.

—— et al., *Leaves from the Tree: J. R. R. Tolkien's Shorter Fiction* (London, 1991). An invaluable collection.

Sidney, Philip, *Defence of Poesie*, ed. A. Feuillerat (1595; Cambridge, 1962 edn.).

Swinfen, A., *In Defence of Fantasy: A Study of the Genre in English and American Literature since 1945* (London, 1984). Influenced by terms of Tolkien's discussion in 'On Fairy Stories': fantasy 'engenders extraordinarily enhanced perception of the nature of the primary world', and explores at length *fantasia* and *imaginativa* (Dante's terms) in the Western tradition. Claims fantasy a serious form of the modern novel.

Tasso, *Discorsi*, trans. M. Cavalchini and I. Samuel (Oxford, 1973).

Teunissen, John J. (ed.), 'Other Worlds: Fantasy and Science Fiction since 1939', *Mosaic*, 13/3–4 (Spring/Summer 1980). A special issue of the periodical, with a wide variety of viewpoints offered by the various contributors.

Todorov, Tzetvan, trans. R. Howards, *The Fantastic: A Structural Approach to a Literary Genre* (Cleveland and London, 1973). A seminal theoretical discussion. But not without problems: see the discussion by Robert M. Philmus, 'Todorov's theory of "The Fantastic": The Pitfalls of Genre Criticism', in *Mosaic* 13/3–4 (Spring/Summer 1980), 71–82.

Tolkien Society, *The First and Second Ages: The 5th Tolkien Society Workshop*, ed. Trevor Reynolds (London, 1992). Four essays, covering *The Silmarillion* as well as *LR*.

Urang, Gunnar, *Shadows of Heaven: Religion and Fantasy in the Fiction of C. S. Lewis, Charles Williams and J. R. R. Tolkien* (London, 1971). Written from a committed Christian position. Examines their fiction's religious background and how it challenges critical and cultural assumptions in the period in which they were writing.

Watt, Ian, *Conrad and the Nineteenth Century* (London, 1980).

Wimsatt, W. K., Jr., *The Verbal Icon: Studies in the Meaning of Poetry* (Lexington, Ky., 1954).

Zipes, J., *Breaking the Magic Spell: Radical Theories of Folk and Fairy Tales* (London, 1979). Compares the Marxist Ernst Bloch and the Christian Tolkien (129–59).

—— *Fairy Tales and the Art of Subversion* (London, 1988). Important theoretical discussion of the social, historical, political contexts of fairy tale, and of its offering a possibility of alternative values, as potentially destabilizing of accepted certainties. Less than total admiration for Lewis and Tolkien.

THE TOLKIEN PHENOMENON

Andrews, Bart, *The Tolkien Quiz-Book: 1,001 Questions about Tolkien's Tales of Middle Earth and Other Fantasies* (London, 1979). With answers. Useful for Trivial Pursuit games.

Beatie, Bruce A., 'The Tolkien Phenomenon: 1954–68', *Journal of Popular Culture*, 3/49 (Spring 1970), 689–73. Groundbreaking article.

Helms, Philip W., *Tolkien's Peaceful War: A History and Exploration of Tolkien Fandom and War* (Highland, Minn., 1994). Discusses Tolkien's reception by protest movements.

Robinson, Nigel and Linda Wilson, *The Tolkien Quiz Book* (London, 1981).

PARODY

Beard, Henry N. and Douglas C. Kennedy, *Bored of the Rings, or, Tolkien Revisited* (New York, 1969). The Harvard Lampoon parody. Fills in many of the omissions in Frodo's passage to maturity. The noticeably sexless world of Tolkien's fiction is rectified (so to speak). See also 'Computer games', below.

Drushel, Richard F., *Annals of the Kings and Rulers of Lower Middle Earth* (1990, 1994). Try http://druid.if.uj.edu.pl/FUN/kroniki.html. An appendix to *Bored of the Rings* available on the Internet. Most of the humour is derived from the playing with names that sound reasonably like Tolkien's but have different resonances – e.g. 'Lutheran Canaveral', 'Turnon, King of the hidden city of Gonadotrophin'.

McNeill, F. and Child, Judith, *The Boggitt* (DELTA 4 Software, CRL

Group Plc, 1986). Available on the Internet. A parody of Melbourne House's adaptation of *The Hobbit*. Illustrated computer-game text adventure. Users on the Internet say 'Technically much better than its predecessor *Bored of the Rings* and very entertaining'.

COMPUTER GAMES

Computer games based on or drawing on the popularity of Tolkien seem to have been available since well before 1979, with names like *Smaug's Lair* and *Carrion Fields*. Since then they have proliferated: over 74 have been recorded since 1980. Some are straightforward versions of *LR* and *The Hobbit*; while some are interactive; some are parody (*Bulbo and the Lizard King*, 1987, *Retarded Creatures and Caverns*, 1989); some use Tolkien's name to sell something a long way removed from the nature of his writing – *Wars of Tolkien* (1995). A list is available on the Internet: http://www.lysator.liu.se./tolkien-games/chronology.html

PERIODICALS

Mythlore: Journal of the Mythopoeic Society, merged with Tolkien Society of America and its Journal (*Tolkien Journal*)
The new Tolkien newsletter
Amon Hen
Andúril: Magazine of Fantasy
Annúminas
Mallorn
Minas Tirith Evening-Star
Orcrist: A Journal of Fantasy in the Arts

Index